I0419503

draw tiny

The mission of Storey Publishing is to serve our customers by publishing practical information that encourages personal independence in harmony with the environment.

North American edition published 2025

Illustrations © 2025 by Anna Tjalsma-Pogorzelec

Text © 2025 by Quarto Publishing Plc

All rights reserved. Hachette Book Group supports the right to free expression and the value of copyright. The purpose of copyright is to encourage writers and artists to produce the creative works that enrich our culture. The scanning, uploading, and distribution of this book without permission is a theft of the author's intellectual property. If you would like permission to use material from the book (other than for review purposes), please contact permissions@hbgusa.com. Thank you for your support of the author's rights.

The information in this book is true and complete to the best of our knowledge. All recommendations are made without guarantee on the part of the author or Storey Publishing. The author and publisher disclaim any liability in connection with the use of this information.

The publisher is not responsible for websites (or their content) that are not owned by the publisher.

Storey books may be purchased in bulk for business, educational, or promotional use. Special editions or book excerpts can also be created to specification. For details, please contact your local bookseller or the Hachette Book Group Special Markets Department at special.markets@hbgusa.com.

Storey Publishing
210 MASS MoCA Way
North Adams, MA 01247
storey.com

Storey Publishing is an imprint of Workman Publishing, a division of Hachette Book Group, Inc., 1290 Avenue of the Americas, New York, NY 10104. The Storey Publishing name and logo are registered trademarks of Hachette Book Group, Inc.

Conceived, edited, and designed by Quarto Publishing, an imprint of The Quarto Group
1 Triptych Place, London SE1 9SH, United Kingdom
quarto.com

QUAR.1176985

ISBN: 978-1-63586-965-1 (paperback)

Printed in China by 1010 Printing International on paper from responsible sources

10 9 8 7 6 5 4 3 2 1

draw tiny

Artful Doodling Activities to Awaken Creativity and Foster Mindfulness

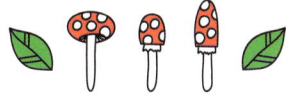

Anna Tjalsma-Pogorzelec
(@licosmoss)

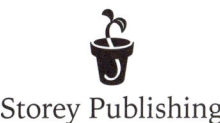

Storey Publishing

Contents

Introduction   6

Tools & materials   7

The projects   8

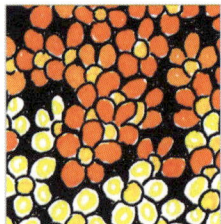 Floral square 8

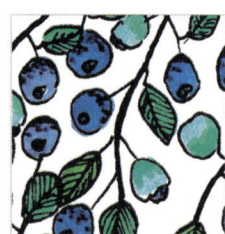 Blueberry mandala 24

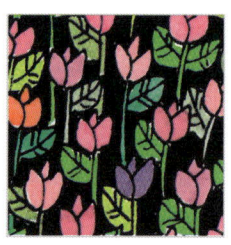 Tulip heart 40

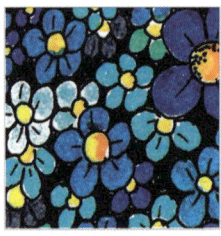 Blue flower mandala 12

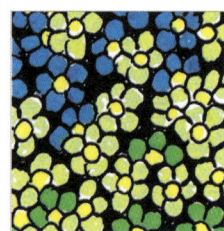 Spring cat 28

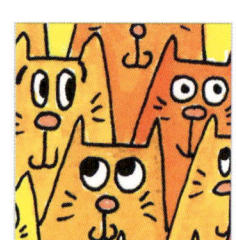 Moon cats 44

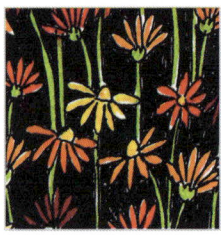 Fall leaf 16

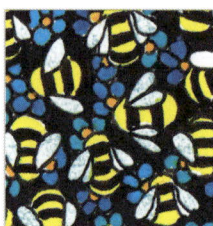 Lightbulb bees 32

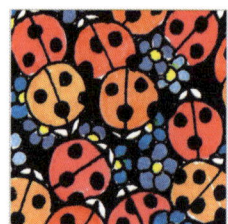 Ladybug heart 48

 Mushroom triangle 20

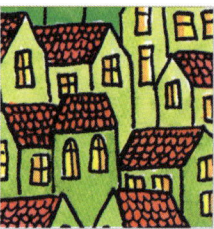 Tulip tree city 36

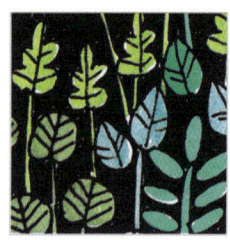 Leafy dog 52

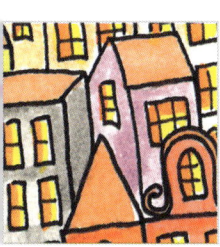 Tiny houses mandala 56

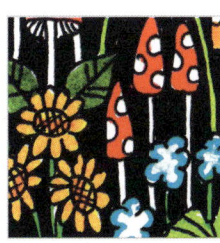 Letter A 72

Drawings to color   88

Acknowledgments   128

Find out more   128

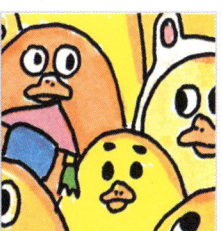 Rubber duckies 60

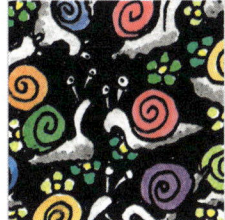 Snails on a leaf 76

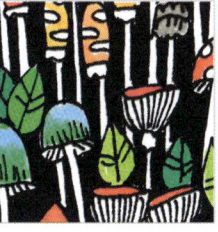 Mushroom moon 64

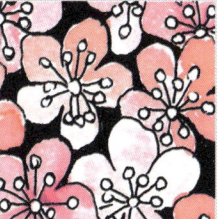 Cherry blossom moon 80

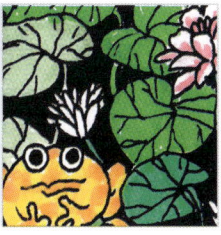 Frog pond 68

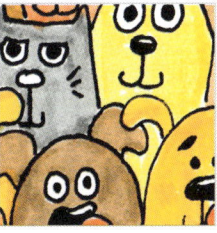 Letter H 84

Introduction

Hi, I'm Anna! I originally come from Poland, but currently live and work in the Netherlands. I have been interested in drawing since I was a child, and my first introduction to art was through coloring books. I could color for hours using crayons or markers, sometimes even watercolor paints. At first, I mostly drew basic shapes like circles or squares. As time passed, the shapes became more and more complex.

My interest in art continued to grow, especially when I became acquainted with famous artists and their techniques—my favorite artists are Vincent van Gogh, Jacek Malczewski, Stanisław Wyspiański, and Tamara de Lempicka. I quickly realized that I did not have such an outstanding talent, but making art allows me to be myself and look at the world differently. Art promotes mindfulness, and through it I can forget about reality and move into a world of dreams. During my studies, I learned about technical drawing and fell in love with lines. I also learned how to draw in miniature, and this laid the foundation for all my tiny drawings. I hope that this book will inspire and encourage you to start your own adventure with art.

For each of the 20 projects in this book, I'll begin by teaching you how to draw the key shapes that comprise each drawing. This is followed by more detailed step-by-step instructions for filling your outline shapes with tiny designs, including advice on coloring in. You can follow along in the book using the practice spaces that accompany the tutorials, and also by filling in a partially-completed outline, which you can then color in using the full color illustration provided for reference. At the back of the book are bonus tear-out pages featuring the completed projects in black and white, which you can color yourself and perhaps even frame! Now, all that's left is to get started—enjoy your journey!

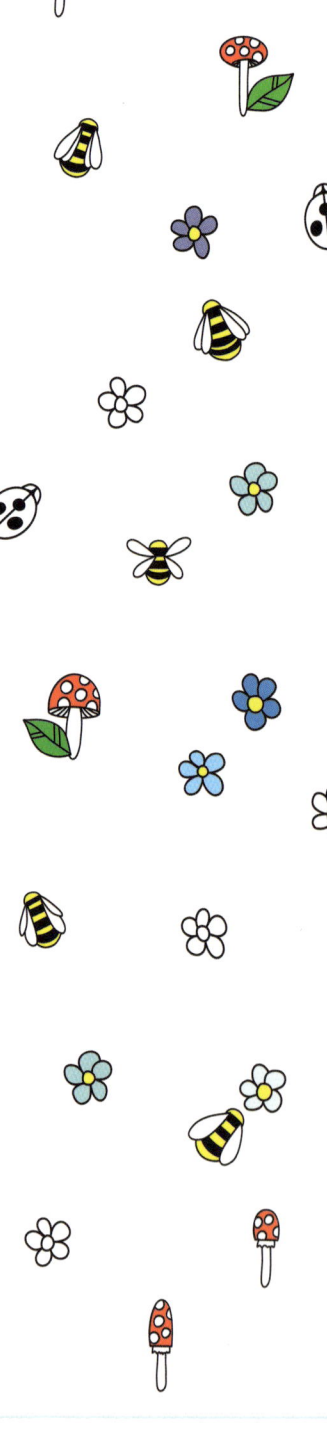

Tools & materials

You don't need any special materials to draw. All you need is an ordinary graphite pencil, colored pencils, fineliners, or markers. Below are some of the basic materials I use.

Paper: There are dedicated pages in the book for drawing and coloring, so you don't need any paper to start drawing. However, if you want to transfer your creations to a slightly larger format, I recommend using heavyweight (200gsm) drawing paper. Such paper will not leak when using markers and you will be able to easily erase the pencil. You should also invest in heavyweight (200gsm) watercolor paper if you want to experiment with watercolor paints.

Black fineliner: Use a black fineliner pen to outline the shapes. It can be of any thickness, from 0.05mm to 2mm. Choose the format that best suits you. My favorites are the Pigment Liner from Staedtler and technical pens from Rotring.

Color fineliners: My favorite color fineliners are Stabilo Point 88 due to the wide range of colors available and the ability to purchase individual pens. The ink is durable and does not quickly discolor when exposed to sunlight.

Color markers: The best markers to use for drawing are water-based (i.e. not alcohol) inks. They do not smear the black fineliner, do not leak, and mix readily without using a blender. Faber-Castell Pitt Artist Pens are my favorite.

In addition, it is helpful to have an eraser, a compass or a small plate for drawing a circle by hand, graphite tracing paper, and a good source of light.

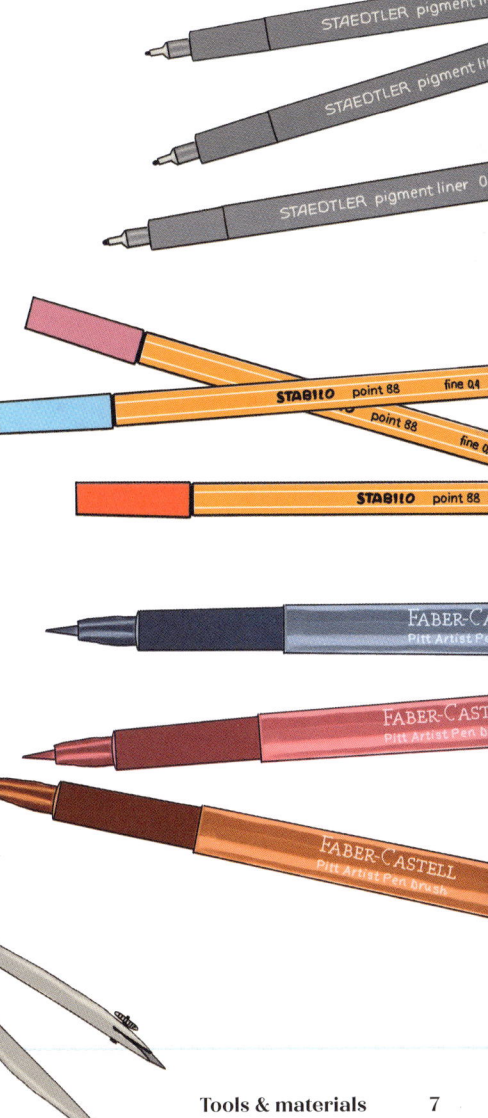

Floral square

I have always been interested in art, geometry, and flowers. One day I decided to try to combine these three elements. All I had to do was choose a form and fill it with flowers. Because I was just starting to rediscover the world of art and learn patience in creating, I chose a square to start my journey. You'll find a range of different shapes and flowers in the projects in this book, but the basic approach to drawing and coloring is always the same.

MATERIALS USED

- Fabriano 200gsm heavyweight paper
- Graphite pencil
- Staedtler 0.2mm black fineliner pen
- Stabilo Point 88 fineliners (colors 19, 30, 40, 44, 48, 50, 54)

Master the basics

Start drawing the flower from its center (1), then add the petals (2-4). Flowers with an odd number of petals usually look nice, especially if you use a simple graphic pattern.

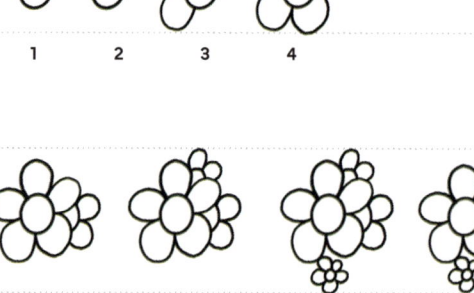

After drawing the first flower, start adding others as shown in steps 1-4. The flowers can fit closely together or even overlap, so the background will be more visible.

Once you have mastered the basic flower and flower cluster, try drawing them smaller and smaller—you can use these blank lines to practice on.

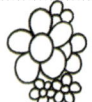

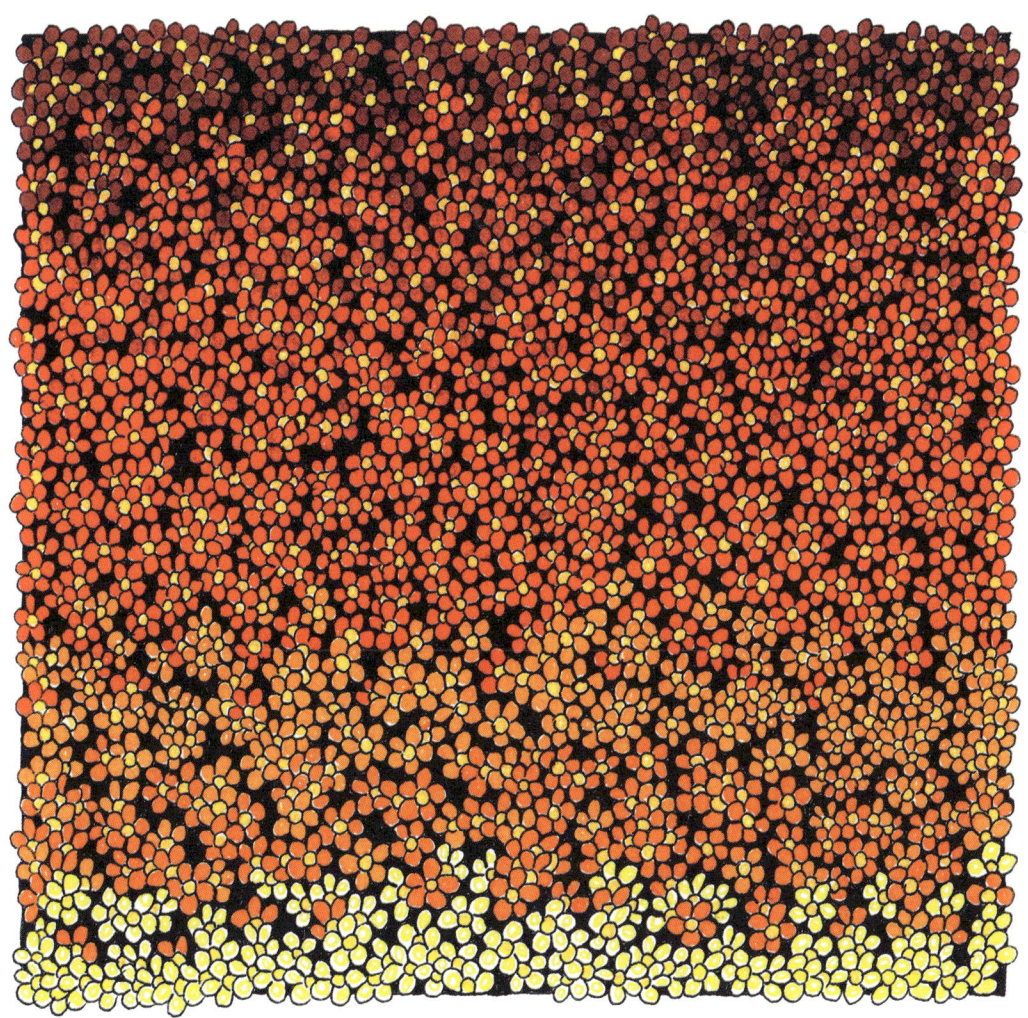

Drawing practice

How to draw and color key shapes

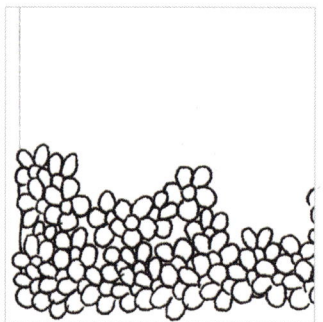
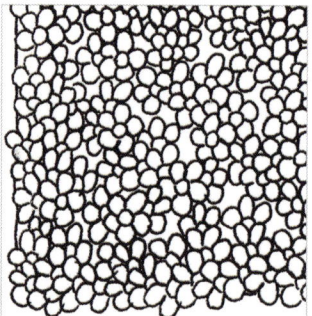
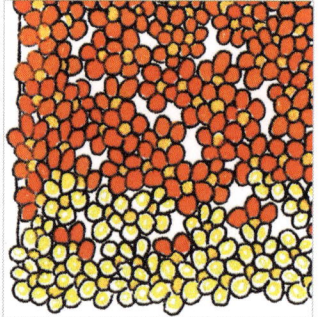
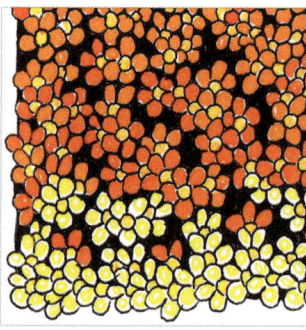

1 Start by drawing your square. Begin to fill it with a simple graphic flower pattern, drawn with a graphite pencil. It's easiest to start from the bottom corner or center baseline. For a more natural drawing, allow some petals to overlap each other and the outline.

2 Once you've filled the entire shape with flowers, go over your flowers again with a black fineliner. Now you can erase any remaining pencil lines.

3 You can grade the colors from the darkest to the lightest or select specific colors to create a colorful meadow; you can use contrasting colors or ones from the same part of the color spectrum to create a calm, harmonious feel. Don't feel obliged to follow my color choices—use whatever you like!

4 I usually choose a black background, as it makes the colors of the flowers stand out more. However, when the flowers are yellow, the background could also be blue, which will create a beautiful contrast.

Practice here

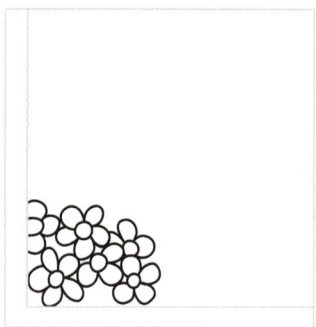
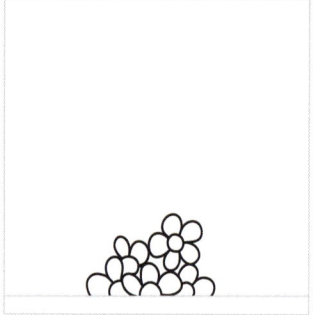
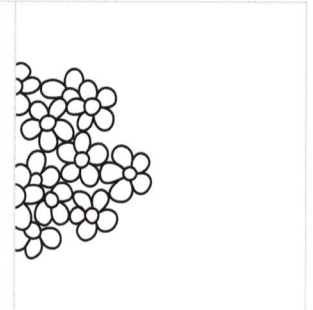

Start filling the flowers from the bottom corner.

Start filling the flowers from the bottom center.

Start filling the flowers from the side of the shape.

TIP Every artist makes mistakes, no matter how experienced they are! Starting your drawings with a graphite pencil will make it easier to correct those mistakes—and give you the freedom to change your mind.

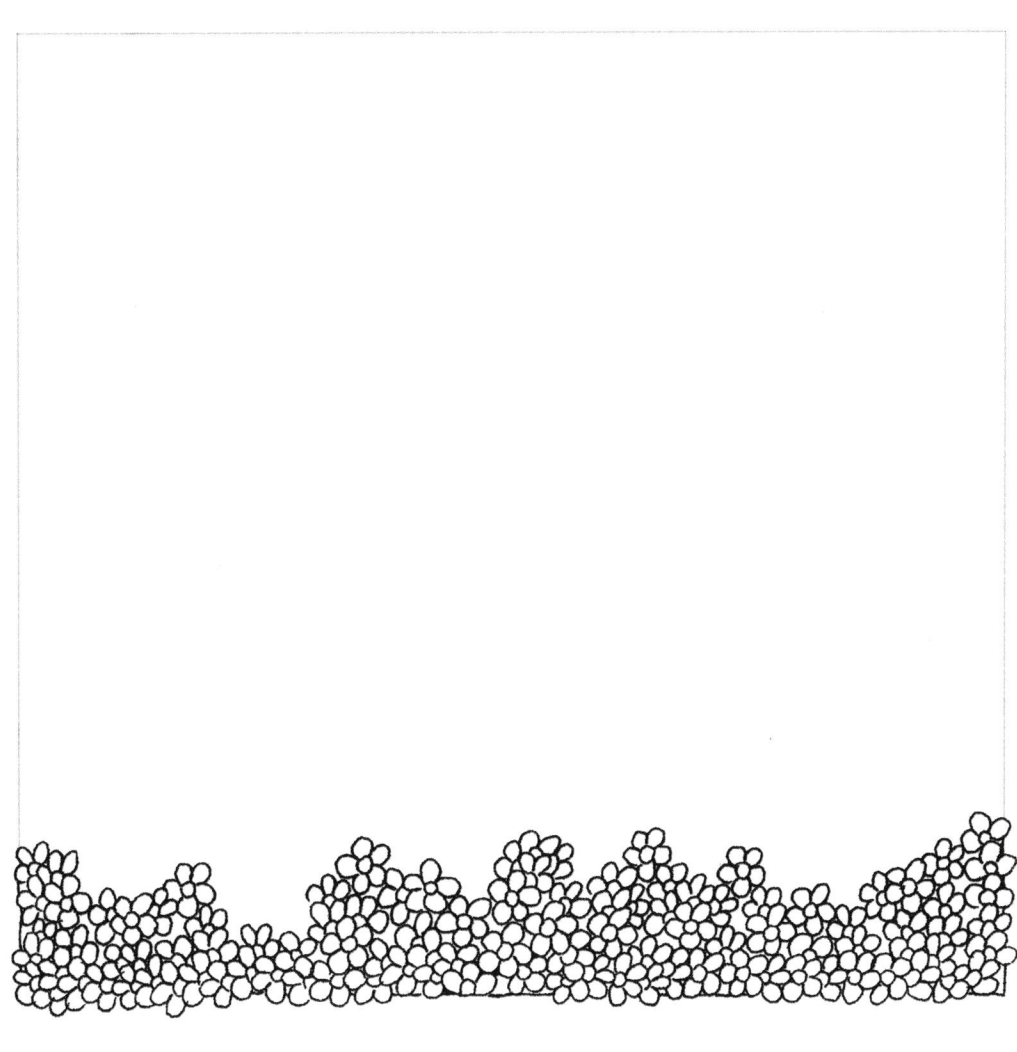

Blue flower mandala

My favorite flowers are forget-me-nots—tiny blue flowers that en masse create a dreamy meadow. This is how I remember them from my grandparents' garden. It will come as no surprise that they appear very often in my works. Next to black, blue is my favorite color—but you can use any color (or, indeed, any flower) you wish.

Every plant has a particular growth pattern, or "habit," so (even though you're not attempting a botanically accurate drawing here) spend time looking at your chosen flower before you start drawing. How big are the largest flowers in relation to the smallest—are they two or three times the size or just a little bit bigger? How many different tones of the same color can you see? Do the flowerheads and petals overlap each other, or do they stand proud on individual stems? Asking yourself questions like this will help you create a drawing that captures the "feel" and character of the flowers.

MATERIALS USED

- Fabriano 200gsm heavyweight paper
- Graphite pencil
- Compass or small plate to draw around
- Rotring Rapidograph 0.2mm technical pen
- Stabilo Point 88 fineliners (colors 11, 13, 30, 31, 32, 41, 44, 57)

Master the basics

The basic shape of these flowers is the same as those used in the Floral Square drawing on page 8, but you can make the flowers look different here by drawing them at various sizes (2-3), and adding details such as lines and shading to the petals and flower centers with your fineliner (4).

Use these blank lines to practice drawing individual flowers and flower clusters, adding detail and shading.

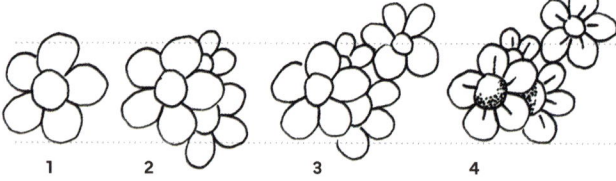

1   2   3   4

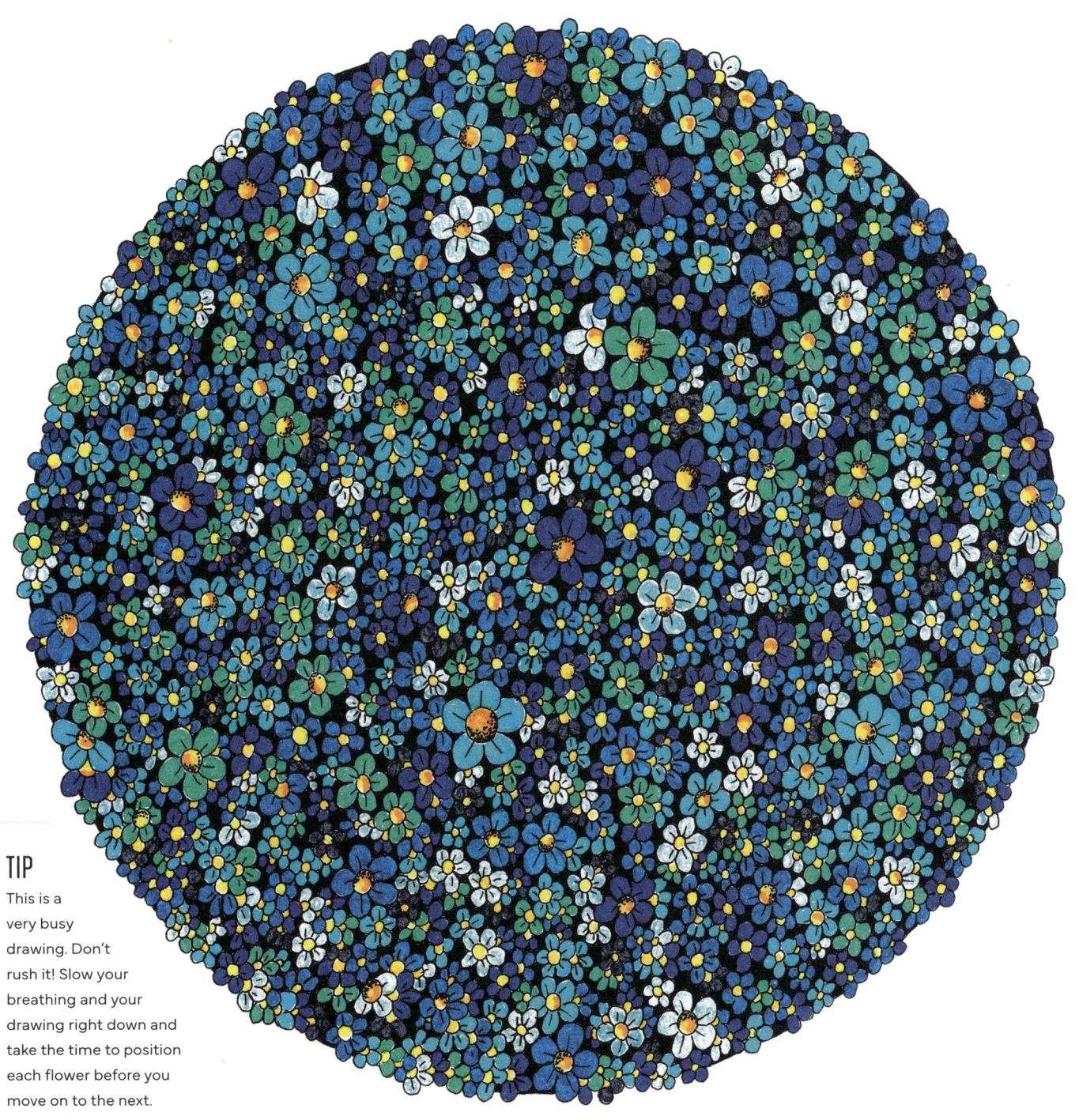

TIP

This is a
very busy
drawing. Don't
rush it! Slow your
breathing and your
drawing right down and
take the time to position
each flower before you
move on to the next.

Drawing practice

How to draw and color key shapes

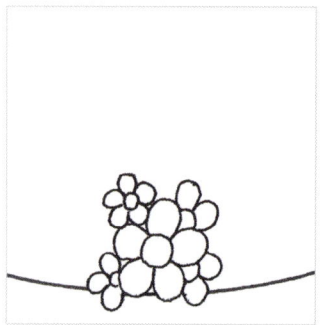

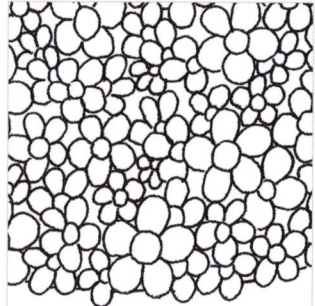

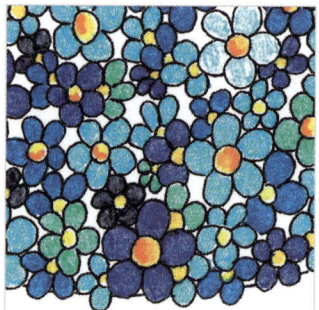

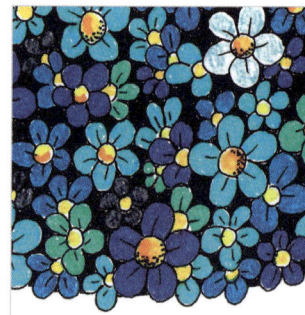

1 Start by using your compass to draw the circle. Using a graphite pencil then a black fineliner, start filling the circle from the bottom. Draw flowers of different sizes, from small to large, and even larger.

2 Continue until you've filled the whole circle. Allow some of the flower petals to go over the edge of the circle in places, and draw some flowers overlapping others, as this creates a softer, more natural-looking effect.

3 Start coloring the flowers. You can use fineliners (as I did), markers, or crayons. With so many similar shapes close together, I find it helps to color in the yellow flower centers first, so that I can keep track of where I am, and then fill in the petal colors around them.

4 Fill in the background, then add details to the flowers, such as veins down the center of the petals and tiny black speckles on some of the flower centers to give texture and imply grains of pollen.

Practice here

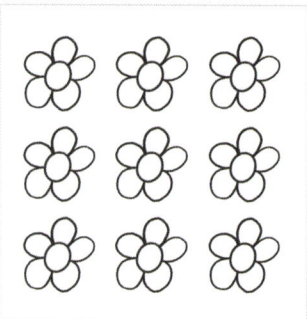

Test different color palettes.

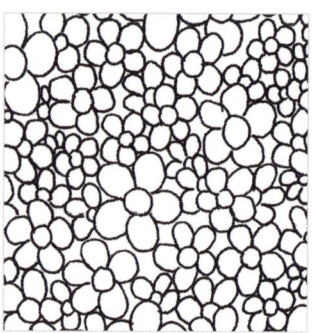

Practice coloring in.

Fill this curved outline from scratch, working from the bottom up.

TIP Stand back and look at your work from a distance from time to time to make sure you're maintaining a good balance of shapes, sizes, and colors.

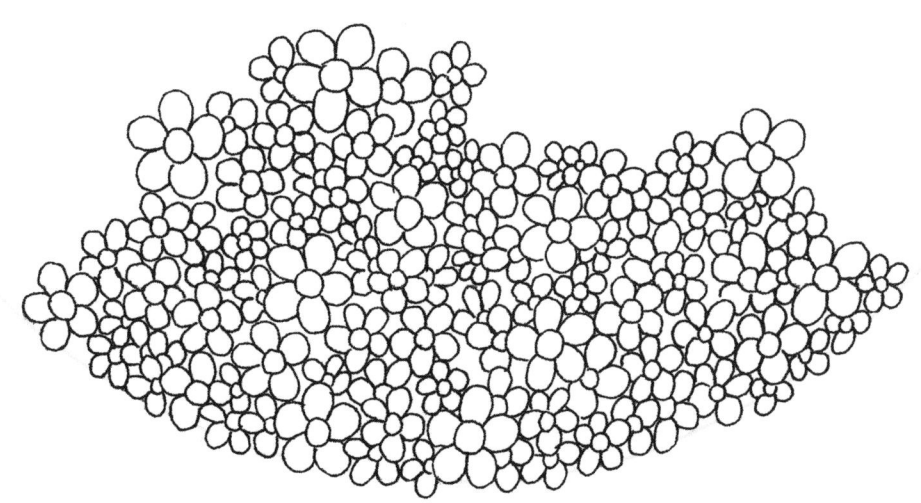

Fall leaf

My favorite season is fall: vibrant colors of yellow, orange, and red, falling leaves and the memory of my dad, whose favorite tree was a birch. He planted it in a corner of the garden and carefully nurtured it for years. Next to the birch tree he dug a pond for ornamental fish and built a bench, where he often sat in the sunshine. Colorful calendulas grew in clumps nearby. This is how I remember him, and that memory was my inspiration for this drawing.

The warm colors in this drawing are all from the same part of the color wheel, which creates a calm, harmonious feel. Try to distribute them fairly evenly, so that you don't end up with blocks of just one color: this keeps your drawing looking free and natural. Experiment with other harmonious color groupings—perhaps cool blues and grays, or yellows through varying shades of green.

MATERIALS USED

- Fabriano 200gsm heavyweight paper
- Graphite pencil
- Rotring 0.2mm technical pen
- Stabilo Point 88 fineliners (colors 19, 30, 40, 43, 44, 48, 54)

Master the basics

Your finished drawing will look more dynamic if you draw the calendulas at different angles, such as the ones shown here. Practice drawing the flowers individually on these practice lines, then try drawing them as a cluster on the bottom line.

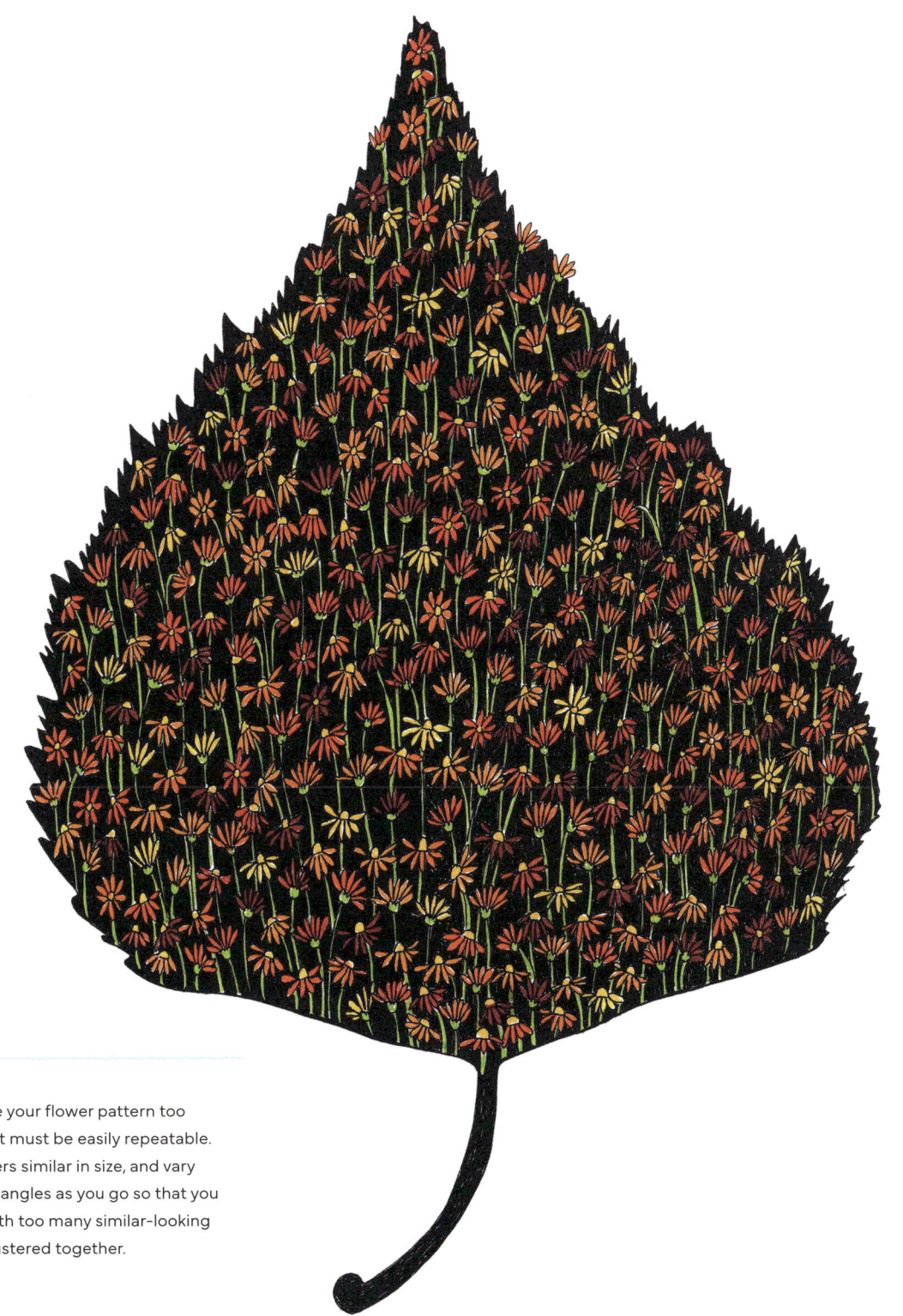

TIP Don't make your flower pattern too complicated—it must be easily repeatable. Keep your flowers similar in size, and vary the shapes and angles as you go so that you don't end up with too many similar-looking flowerheads clustered together.

Drawing practice

How to draw and color key shapes

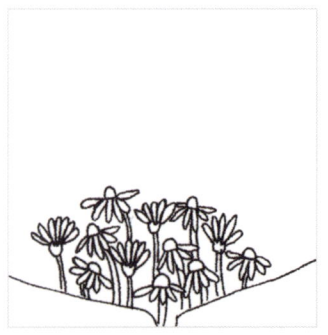 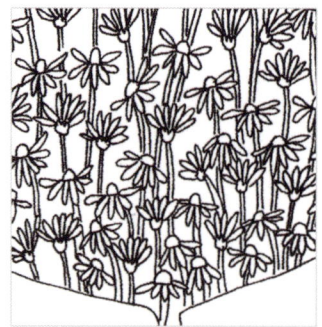 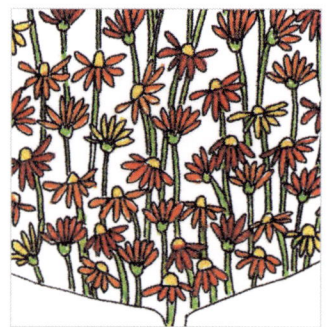 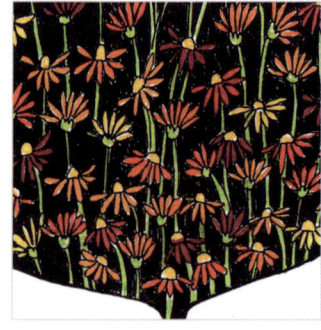

1 Start by drawing your birch leaf outline by hand, then begin filling the leaf with flowers. I chose calendula, but you can use any fall flower you like. As always, start filling from the bottom of your shape.

2 Continue until you've filled the whole leaf with flowers. Vary the flower shapes and the angles of the stems, since this will help to make your drawing look more lively. Go over your pencil lines with a black fineliner.

3 Now you can start coloring! Use just one or two colors to begin with and distribute them fairly evenly across the leaf shape. Use your remaining colors to complete the design. Stand back from your work at regular intervals to assess the overall color balance.

4 Leave the background until the end to keep the drawing clean. If you fill in the background before coloring the flowers, there is a good chance that the ink will transfer to the flowers and their colors will become smoky.

Practice here

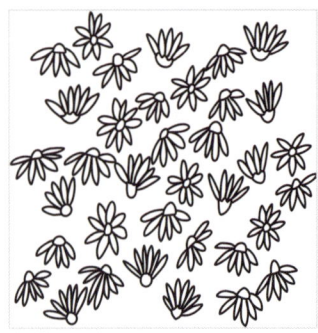 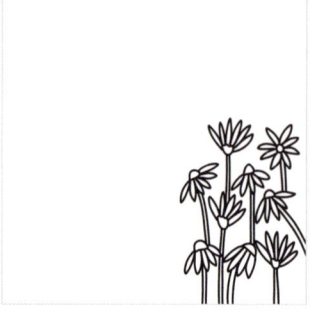 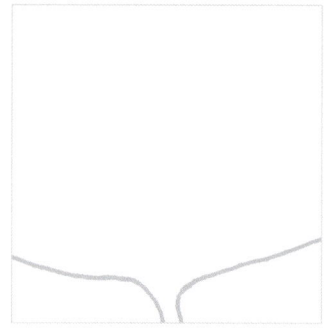

Add the stems to these flowerheads.

Practice drawing both flowers and stems.

Fill this outline with flowers.

TIP Drawing the flowers vertically in your leaf and allowing each stem to blend into the flowerheads above and below, will make the calendulas look like they are connected on long floral chains.

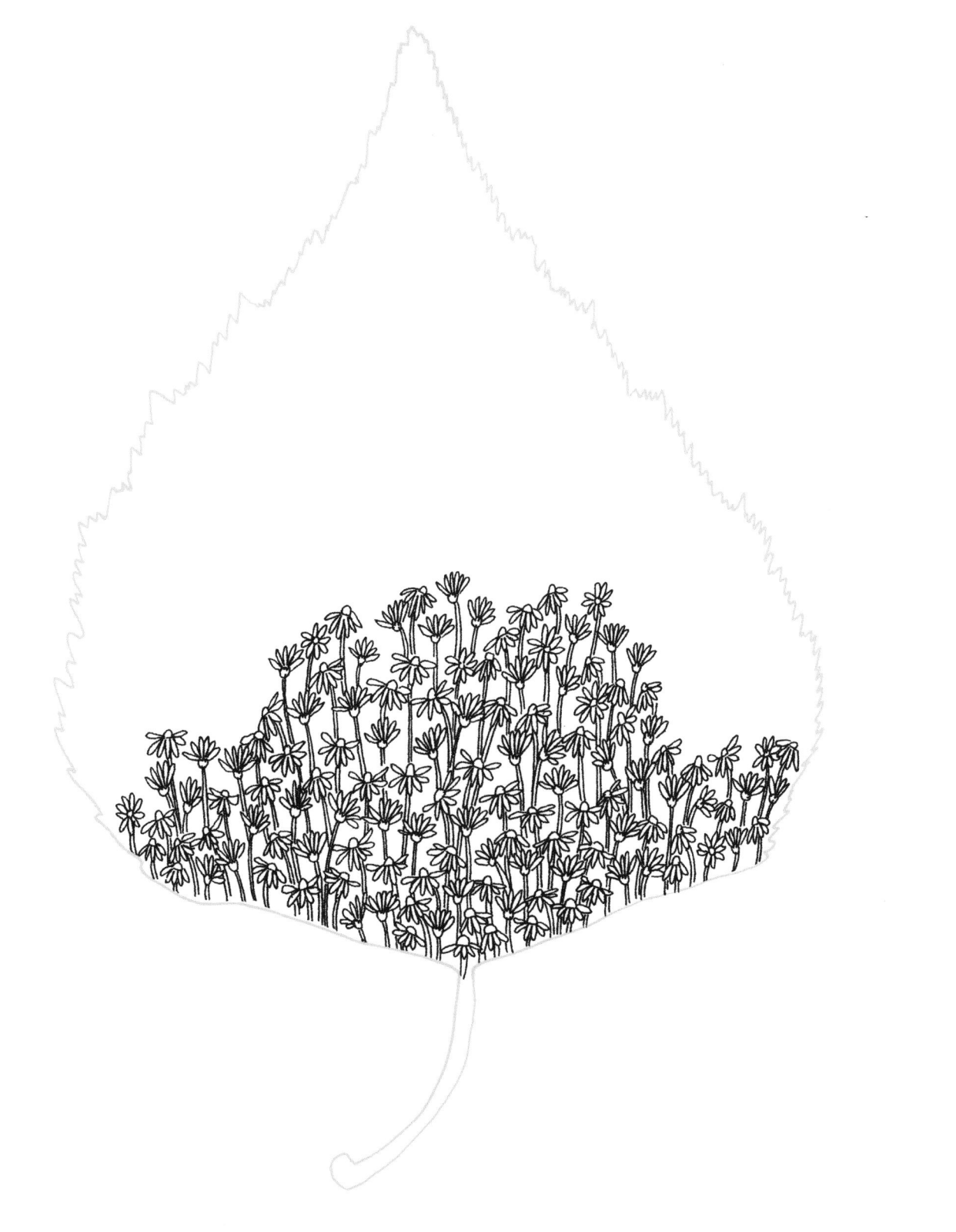

Mushroom triangle

I have to tell you a secret: I come from a family of mushroom pickers. I was taken to pick mushrooms when I was just a few months old and, as a child, was taught to recognize which ones are edible and which ones are poisonous. I owe my knowledge about mushrooms to my parents. To this day, every fall I go to the forest to look for mushrooms.

This drawing could be straight out of an illustrated fairytale—the classic fly agaric mushrooms (red caps with white dots) would make a whole town of little fairy houses! The main color contrast is between the complementary colors of red (for the mushroom caps) and green (for the leaves). There's also a secondary contrast between the white dots on the mushrooms and the deep, black background.

MATERIALS USED

- Fabriano 200gsm heavyweight paper
- Graphite pencil
- Staedtler 0.1mm black fineliner pen
- Faber-Castell Pitt Artist Pens (colors 112, 121, 174, 219, 264)

Master the basics

These mushroom shapes are very simple—either a semi-circular cap or a more elongated oval, rather like a popsicle. Start by drawing a single mushroom, as shown here in steps 1-5. Next, construct other mushrooms around it, varying the angles of the stalks to create more visual interest. Finally, add some leaves.

Use the blank lines here to follow the step by step on the top row, then practice drawing these variations.

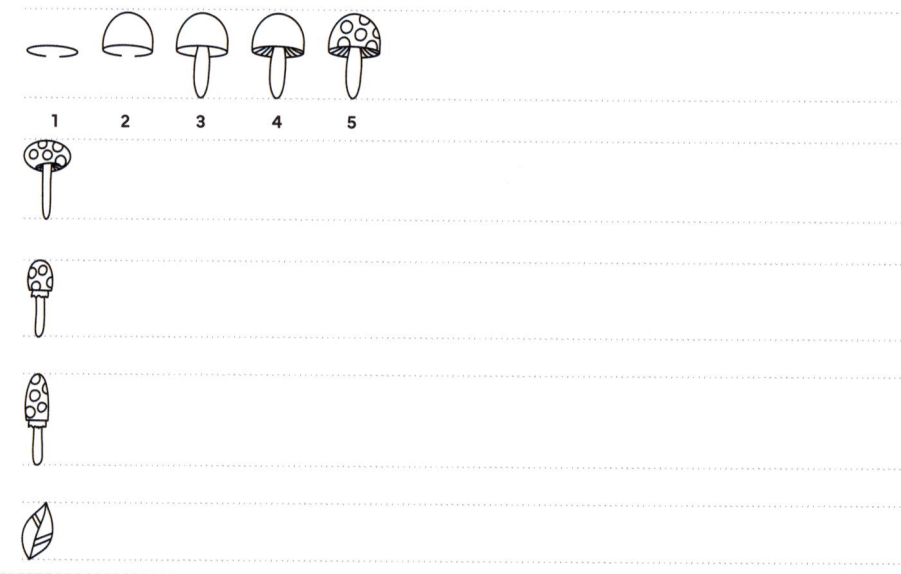

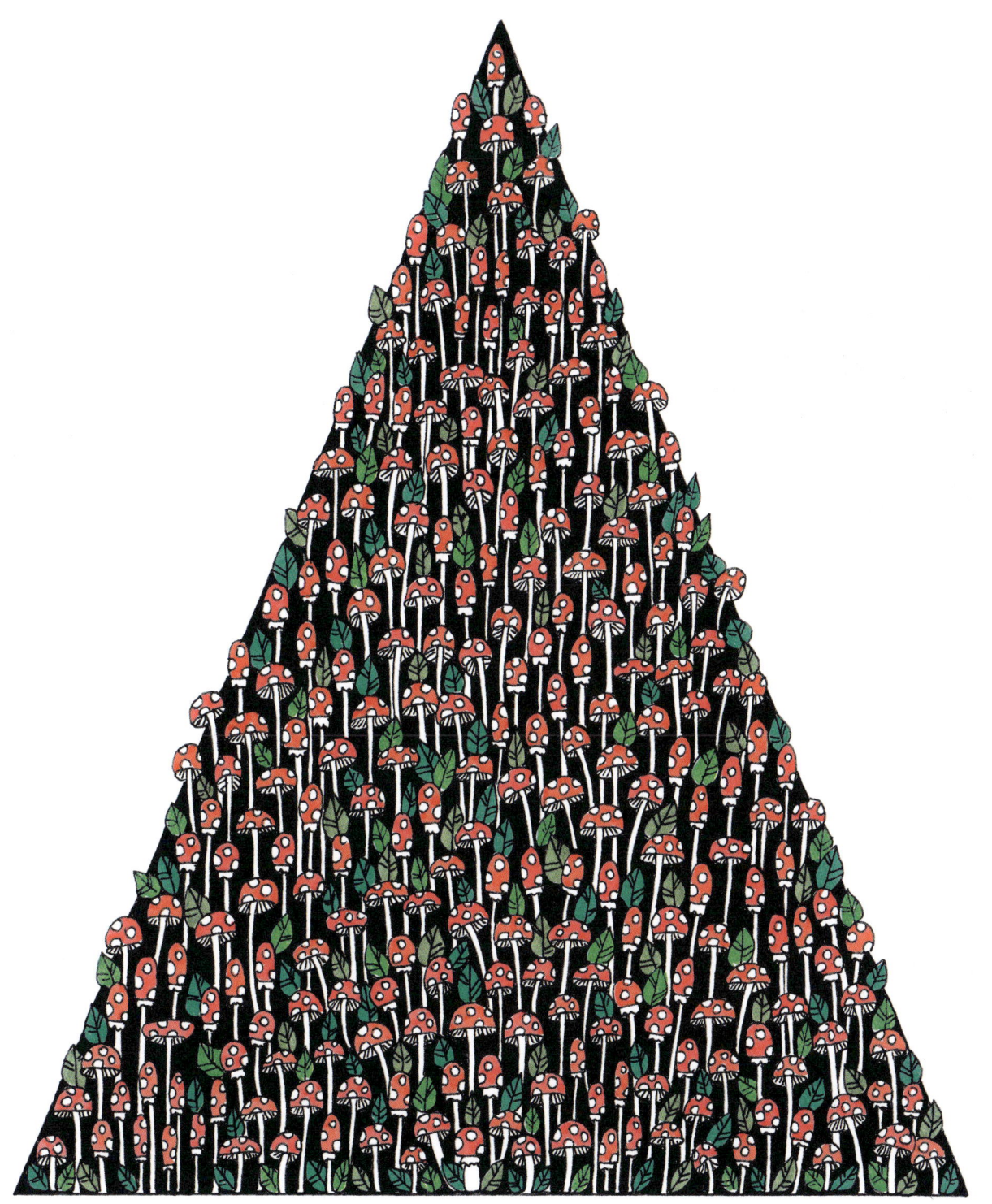

Drawing practice

How to draw and color key shapes

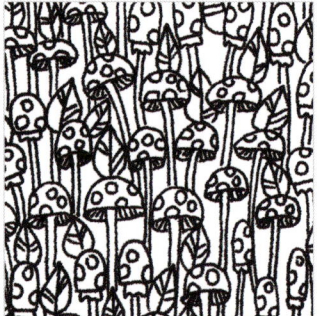  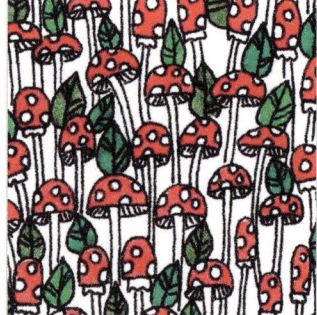 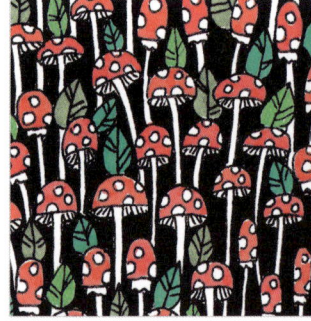

1 Start by drawing your triangle. Begin filling it at the bottom and work your way up. Place small leaves between the mushrooms for better color contrast and allow some shapes to protrude ever so slightly beyond the edge of the outline.

2 Continue until you've completely filled the triangle. Go over your pencil lines with a black fineliner pen, then start coloring. Color the mushroom caps first in a vibrant red, remembering to leave the dots white!

3 Add two or three different shades of green for the leaves, leaving the stalks and the dots on the mushroom caps white.

4 Use black to fill in the background. You will see how amazing the bright toadstools look in contrast!

Practice here

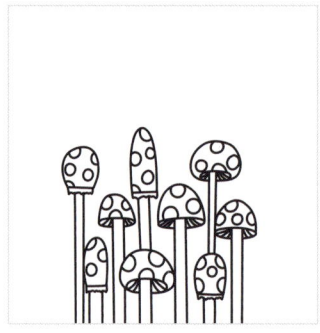 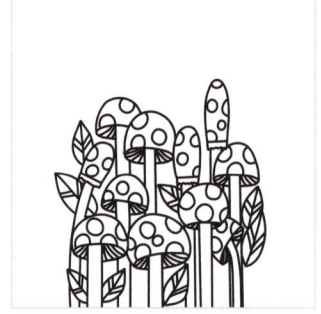 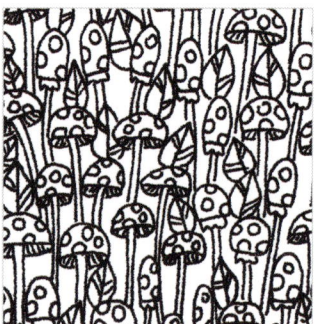

Add more mushrooms to this box, drawing them close to each other and at different heights.

Now draw some of the mushrooms behind each other and overlapping. Add leaves.

Color these mushrooms. You could even try a different color palette here!

TIP Curve some of the stalks slightly so that your drawing doesn't look too linear and regimented.

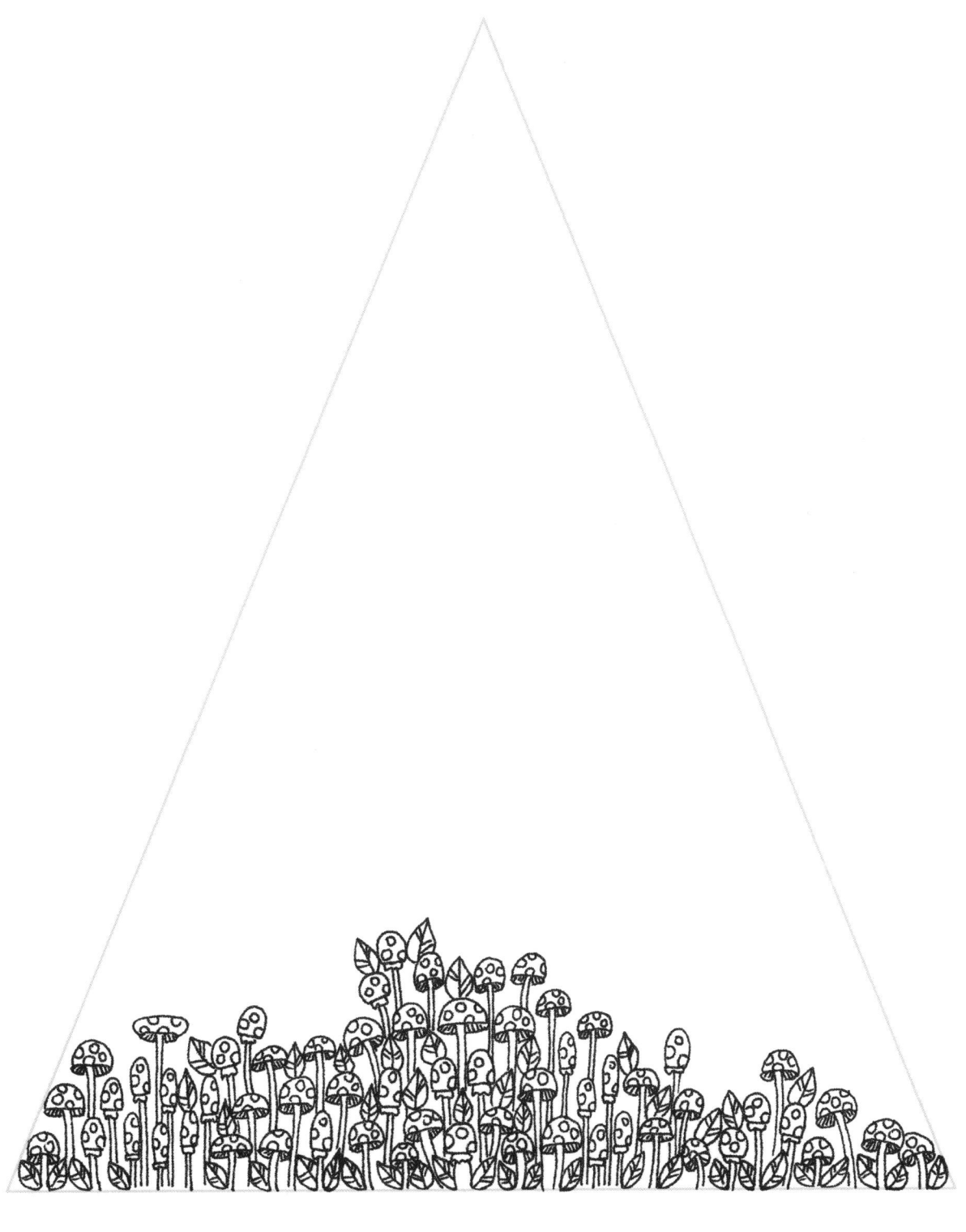

Blueberry mandala

Is there anything better than blueberries? I can eat them for breakfast, lunch, and dinner! Every year I look forward to berry season. You can buy them fresh at a market stall or pick them yourself. Not far from my parents' house there is a forest full of blueberries. The best time to harvest is early morning, when there are fewer mosquitoes and the heat of the day has not yet set in. The blueberry mandala is almost an ode to my favorite fruit.

    This drawing is all about circles and curves: the round berries echo the circular shape within which they're contained, while the curving branches create a gently flowing composition that feels very natural. Straight shapes would look very angular and spiky within the frame and create a very different mood.

MATERIALS USED

- Fabriano 200gsm heavyweight paper
- Graphite pencil
- Compass or small plate to draw around
- Staedtler 0.5mm black fineliner pen
- Faber-Castell Pitt Artist Pens (colors 120, 143, 154, 156, 161, 167, 264)

Master the basics

Blueberries are a simple round shape, which makes them easy to draw repeatedly. Change their size and color to differentiate between ripe (top) and unripe berries (below).

The branches connecting the berries can be drawn as thin wavy lines. Draw the leaves as shown here in steps 1-3, perhaps changing their color slightly to add interest to your drawing.

Any round berry would work in this mandala. Why not try drawing holly, mistletoe, gooseberries, or blackcurrants on these practice lines?

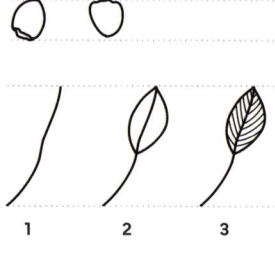

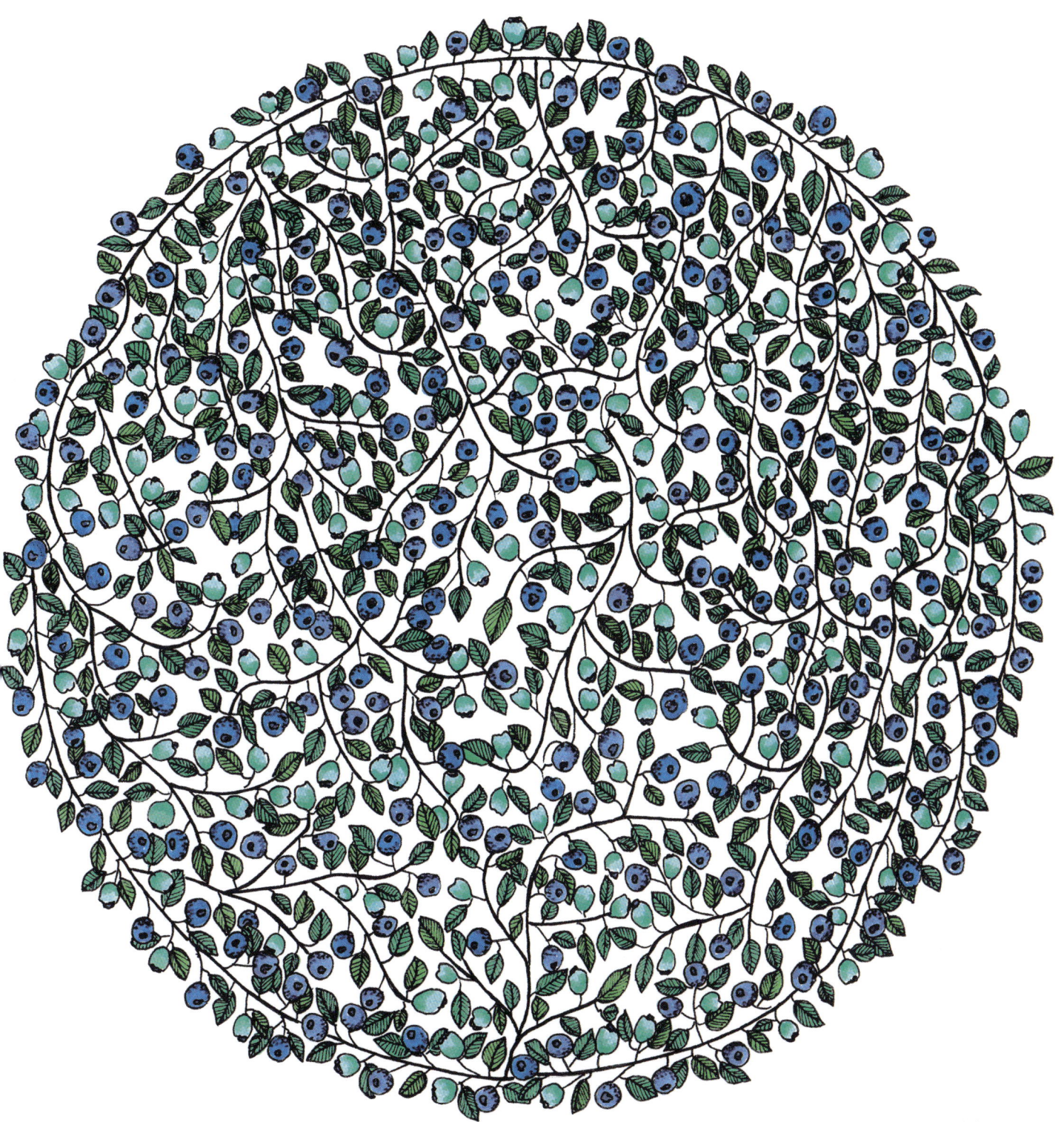

Drawing practice

How to draw and color key shapes

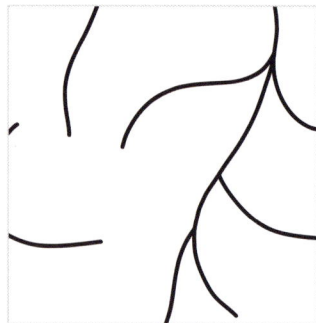

1 Start by using your compass to draw the circle. Then draw the first branch using a graphite pencil. When you've filled the first branch, add the next. When you're happy, go over the pencil lines with a black fineliner.

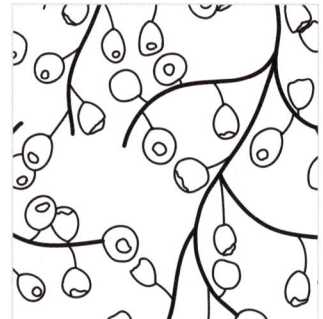

2 Add the berries branching out from the main stems, with a little circle at the end of each one. The berries should look slightly different in size and shape.

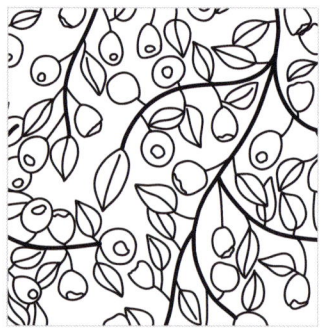

3 Then add in the leaves, overlapping some and tucking others away behind the berries.

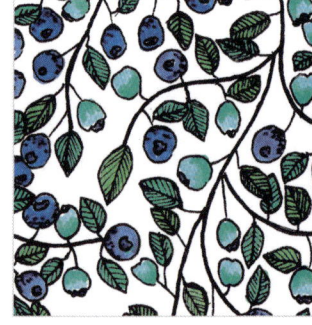

4 I chose dark blue for ripe berries and green and light blue for berries that still need to ripen. If you only want ripe fruit, use only blue—and select a darker blue for the little circle at the tip of each fruit. You can also add some details to the leaves if you wish, but it's not essential. This time, don't fill in the background with any color.

Practice here

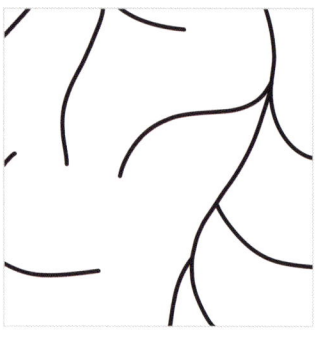

Add blueberries and leaves to these branches.

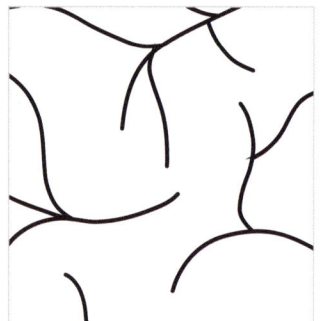

Practice drawing and coloring blueberries on these branches.

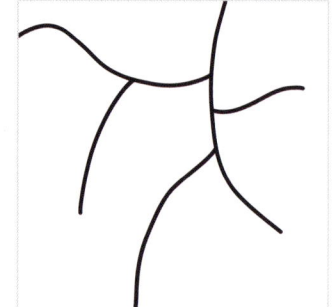

Try drawing and coloring other types of berries.

TIP Draw gentle curves for the branches—there's no set rule, so just let your hand meander slowly over the paper. Draw the branches from the bottom of the circle, allowing some to follow the outline, and work up. Allow some leaves and berries to overlap the branches at the edge of the circle to create a softer, more natural outline.

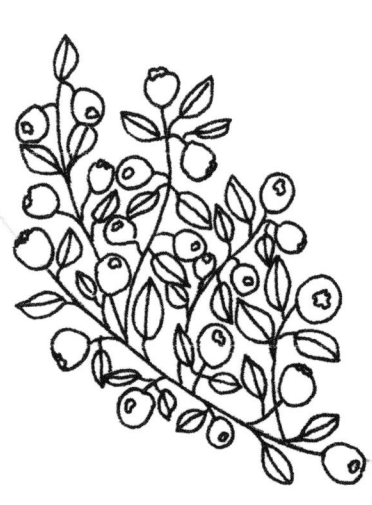

Spring cat

I love cats (I have a cat myself—her name is Blue, and she has beautiful gray-silver fur and emerald-green eyes), so the inspiration for this next drawing was very simple. I also took inspiration from the season of spring: to me, there's nothing more beautiful in spring than the sight of green grass and a blue sky. To combine the two I decided to "grade" the colors. Color grading involves using one color in several shades, ranging from darkest to lightest, or vice versa. As you work from one shade to the next, connect them in such a way that they do not create rigid stripes in the drawing, but instead "merge" with each other.

For your first attempt, it's easiest to color grade on a basic shape, so we'll use the flower design we learned in the Floral Square project (page 8).

MATERIALS USED

- Fabriano 200gsm heavyweight paper
- Graphite pencil
- Staedtler 0.1mm black fineliner pen
- Faber-Castell Pitt Artist Pens (colors 110, 112, 120, 143, 146, 148, 154, 167, 170, 171, 174)

Master the basics

First, choose your color palette. This could be shades of yellow, green, or blue, or a combination of all of them.

Try all the colors on a separate sheet of paper. This way you can easily arrange them from darkest to lightest, or vice versa.

When you feel you've experimented enough, color in these three rows with your favorite color grades.

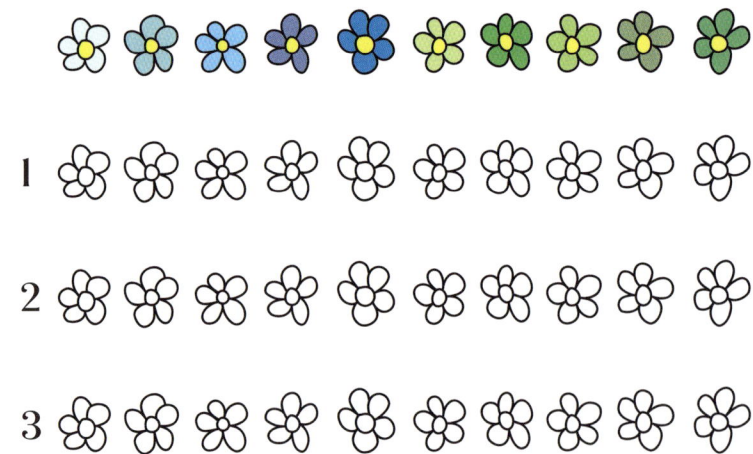

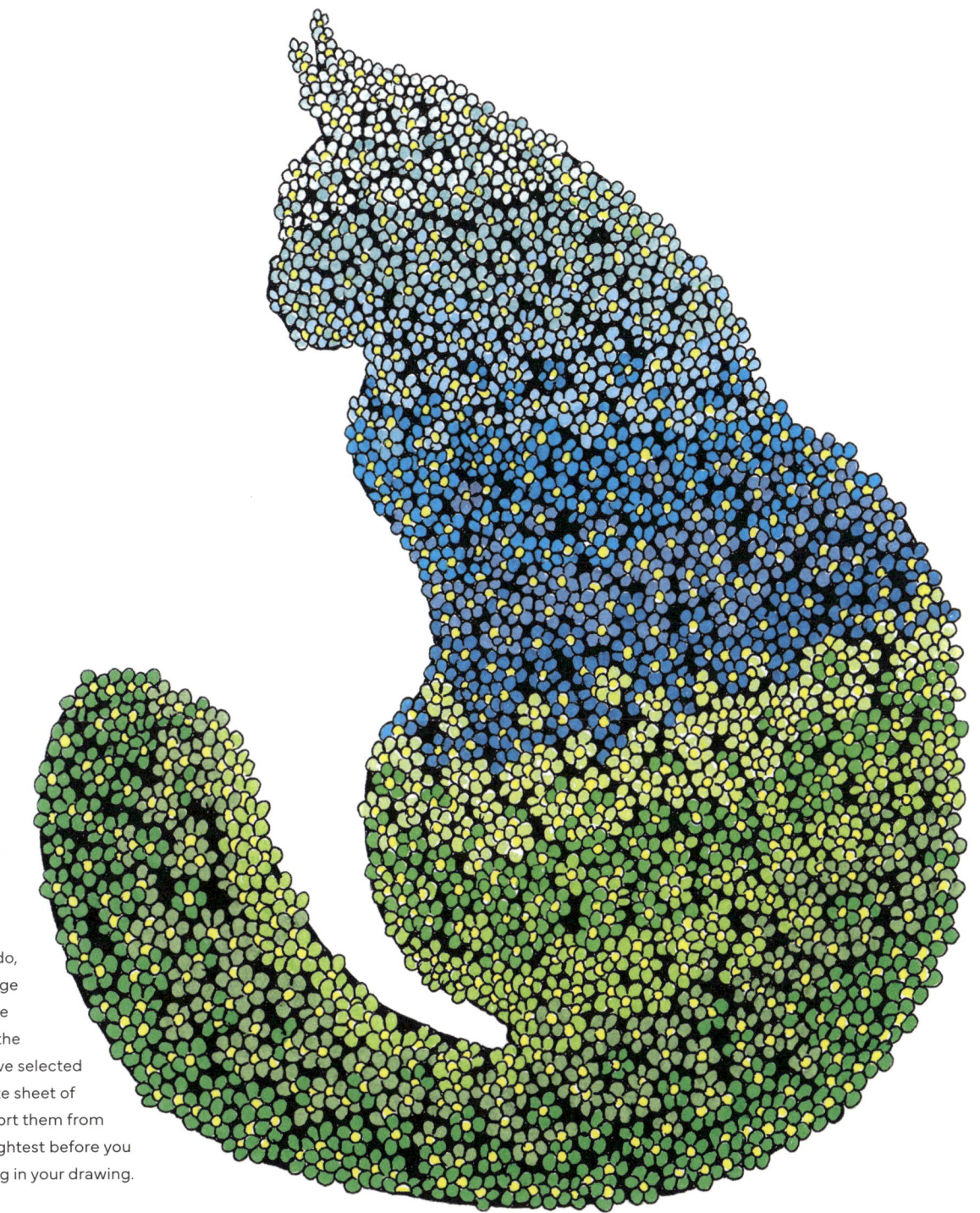

TIPS Color grading is not easy to do, so I encourage you to try the intensity of the shades you've selected on a separate sheet of paper and sort them from darkest to lightest before you start coloring in your drawing.

Drawing practice

How to draw and color key shapes

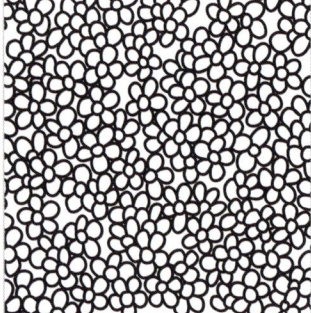
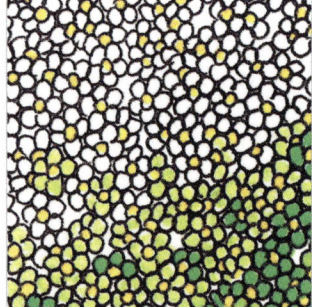
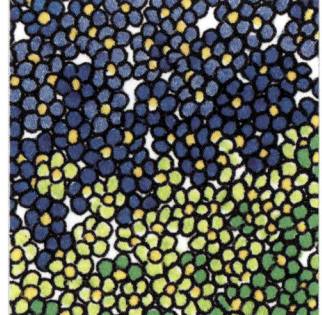
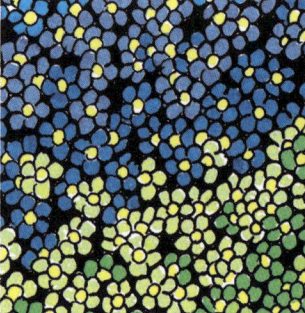

1 Start by drawing the cat outline. Fill it with small flowers using a graphite pencil then a black fineliner. The easiest way to start is by filling in the tail. Tuck some flowers behind others and overlap them, rather than drawing every flower in its entirety.

2 Color the centers yellow or orange first, then fill two or three rows of flowers with the first color you've selected; I started with a fairly dark green. Remember not to create regular stripes, but color a few flowers a row or two above and below.

3 Move to the next color—a mid-green, in my case. Repeat the process, moving through all the greens in your selection until you've applied the lightest shade.

4 About halfway up the cat's body, switch to your second color group—blue, in my case, working from darkest to lightest. I worked from a dark to a mid-tone blue and finally to a light turquoise. When you've finished coloring, fill in any gaps in the background in black.

Practice here

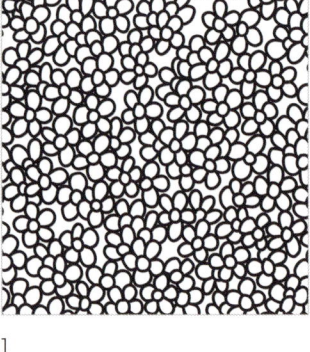
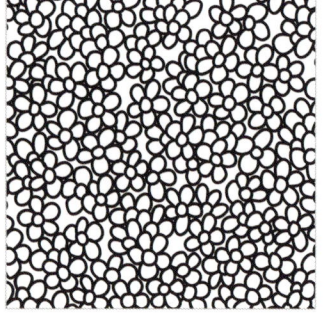

1

2

3

Color the flowers in each of these boxes using your three favorite color grades from the previous page.

TIP Take your time coloring the flower centers—it's easy to lose track of where you are and find you've colored in a petal by mistake!

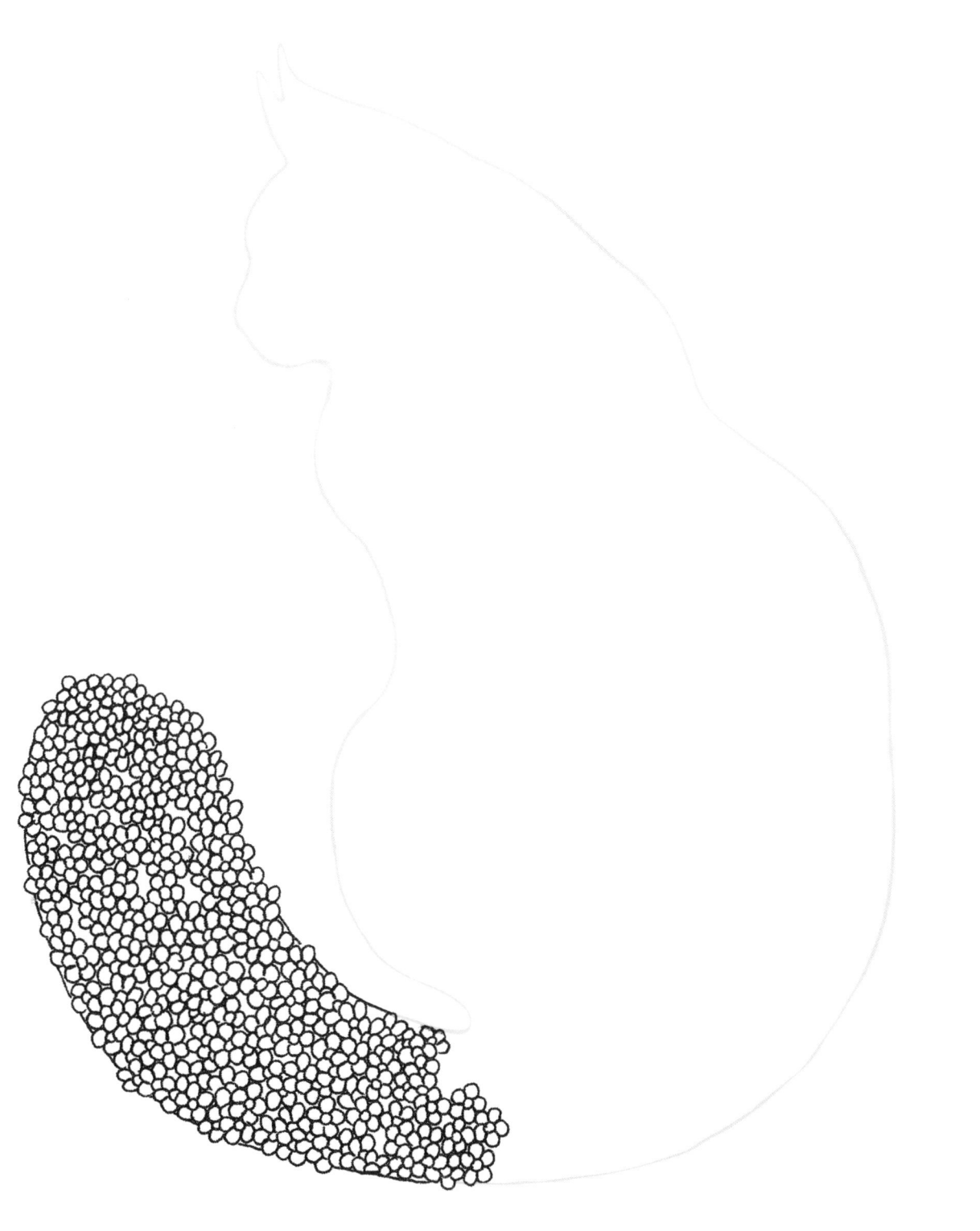

Lightbulb bees

This drawing is my attempt to represent what should be a "lightbulb" or "eureka" moment for us all about the state of nature. Bees play a key role in the ecological system: they are responsible for pollinating flowers, enabling the formation of fruits and seeds, and without them it would be difficult to find food for most animal species. Unfortunately, bee populations around the world have been decreasing dramatically for many years. We should protect our little allies so that our world continues to delight us with its beauty, so take care of your gardens and plant more flowers that will feed our bees with nectar.

One of the keys to creating a lively, interesting drawing is to think about the scale of the different elements: here, for example, I made the bees roughly twice the size of the flowers, so that they stand out as being the most important thing. I also varied the angles, so that the bees are not all facing in the same direction.

MATERIALS USED

- Fabriano 200gsm heavyweight paper
- Graphite pencil
- Staedtler 0.2mm and 1mm black fineliner pens
- Faber-Castell Pitt Artist Pens (colors 107, 109, 110, 120, 143, 146, 148, 153, 199, 232, 233, 235)

Master the basics

Start with the bee's wings, placing them roughly at right angles to each other (1). Then draw the bee's body in between—it's roughly a teardrop shape (2). Color in the body, then add the bee's black stripes to finish (3).

You can draw bees in a few different ways, such as the variations shown here with the wings in different positions. Use these blank lines as practice space for the bee variations.

1   2   3

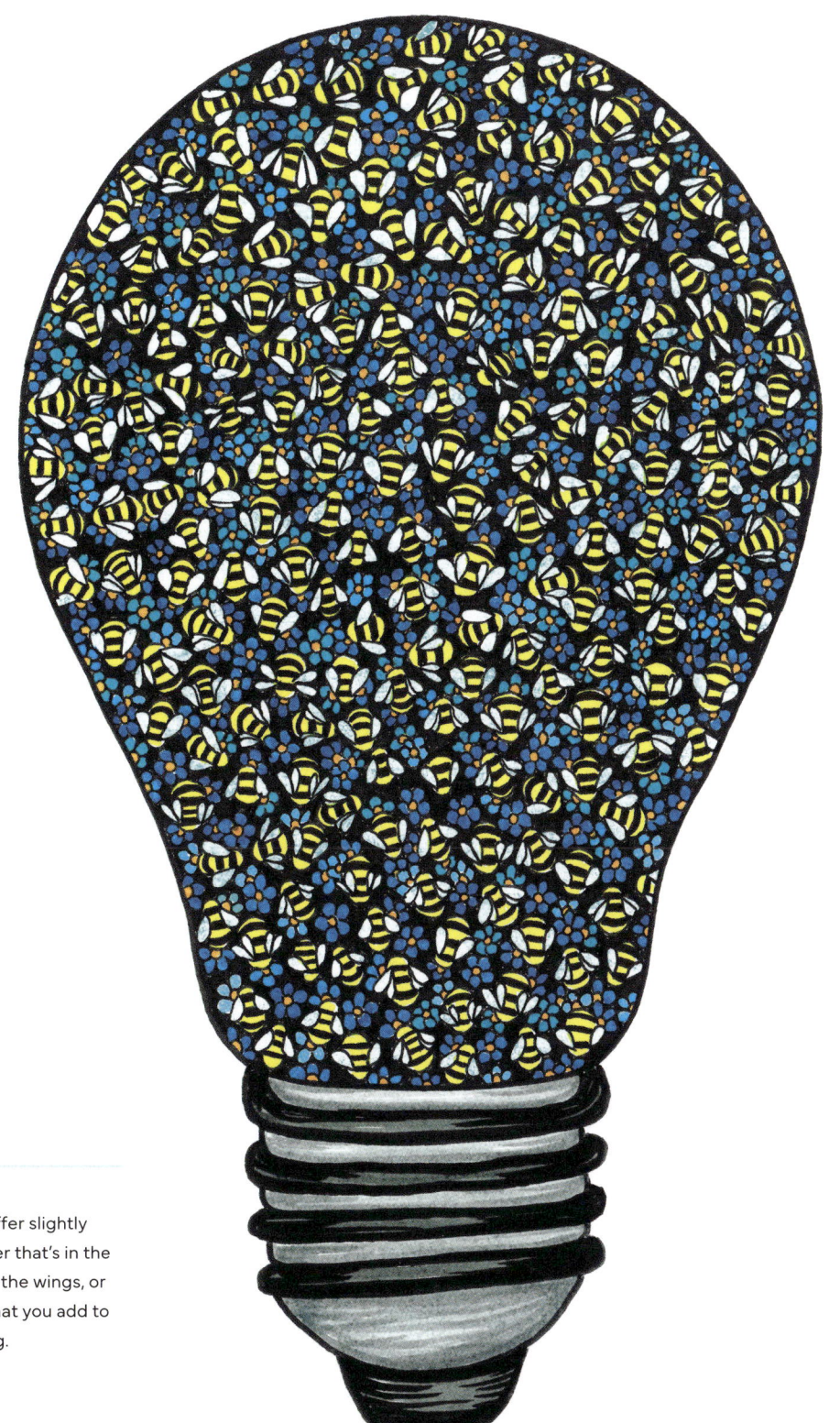

TIP The bees should differ slightly from each other, whether that's in the direction they're facing, the wings, or the number of stripes that you add to the bodies after coloring.

Drawing practice

How to draw and color key shapes

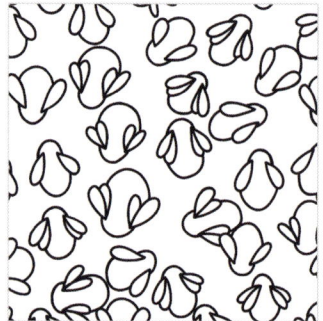 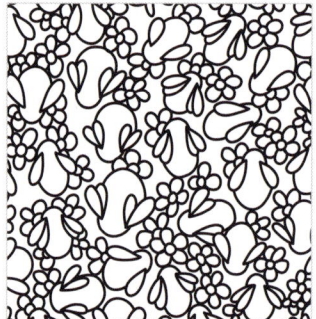 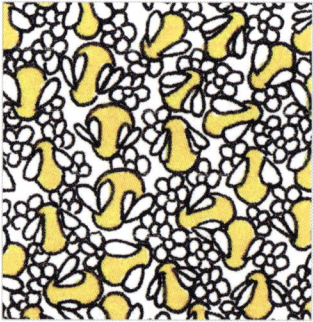 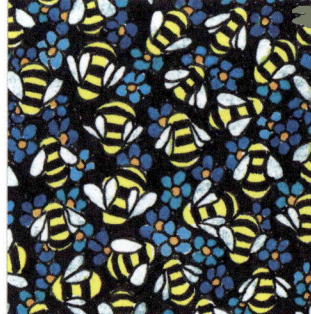

1 Start by drawing the lightbulb outline. Then begin filling the bulb with bees, starting at the bottom and working your way up, using a graphite pencil then a black fineliner. Draw the bee's wings first, then the body.

2 When you've drawn a few bees at different angles and spacings, fill in the spaces in between with little five-petaled flowers, as in the Blue Flower Mandala on page 12—because what would a bee be without flowers?

3 Once you've filled the bulb, you can start coloring. The bees' bodies are the largest and most important elements, so start with those. Then shade the coils of the lightbulb, alternating between graphite pencil and a 1mm black fineliner pen.

4 Color the flowers in various shades of blue and the flower centers in orange. Leave the bees' wings white. Color in the bees' black stripes. Fill in any spaces in the background in black, too; this will really make the yellows and blues "pop."

Practice here

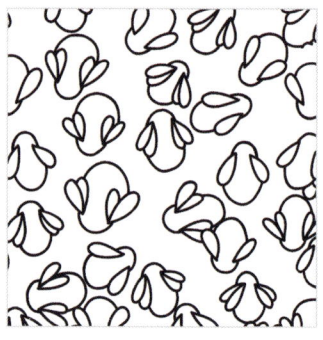 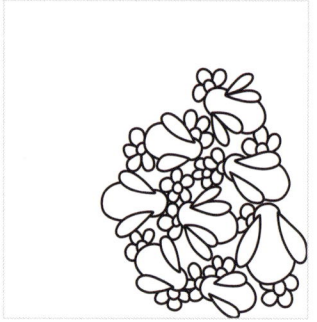 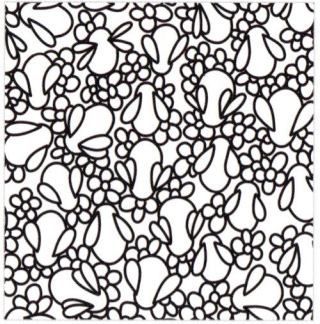

Fill in the spaces in between these bees with flowers.

Continue filling this box with bees and flowers.

Color this box and add the bees' stripes.

TIP Create shading on the coils of the lightbulb by using three colors: light gray, dark gray, and black. By repeating the same color in the same place, you will obtain additional color depth.

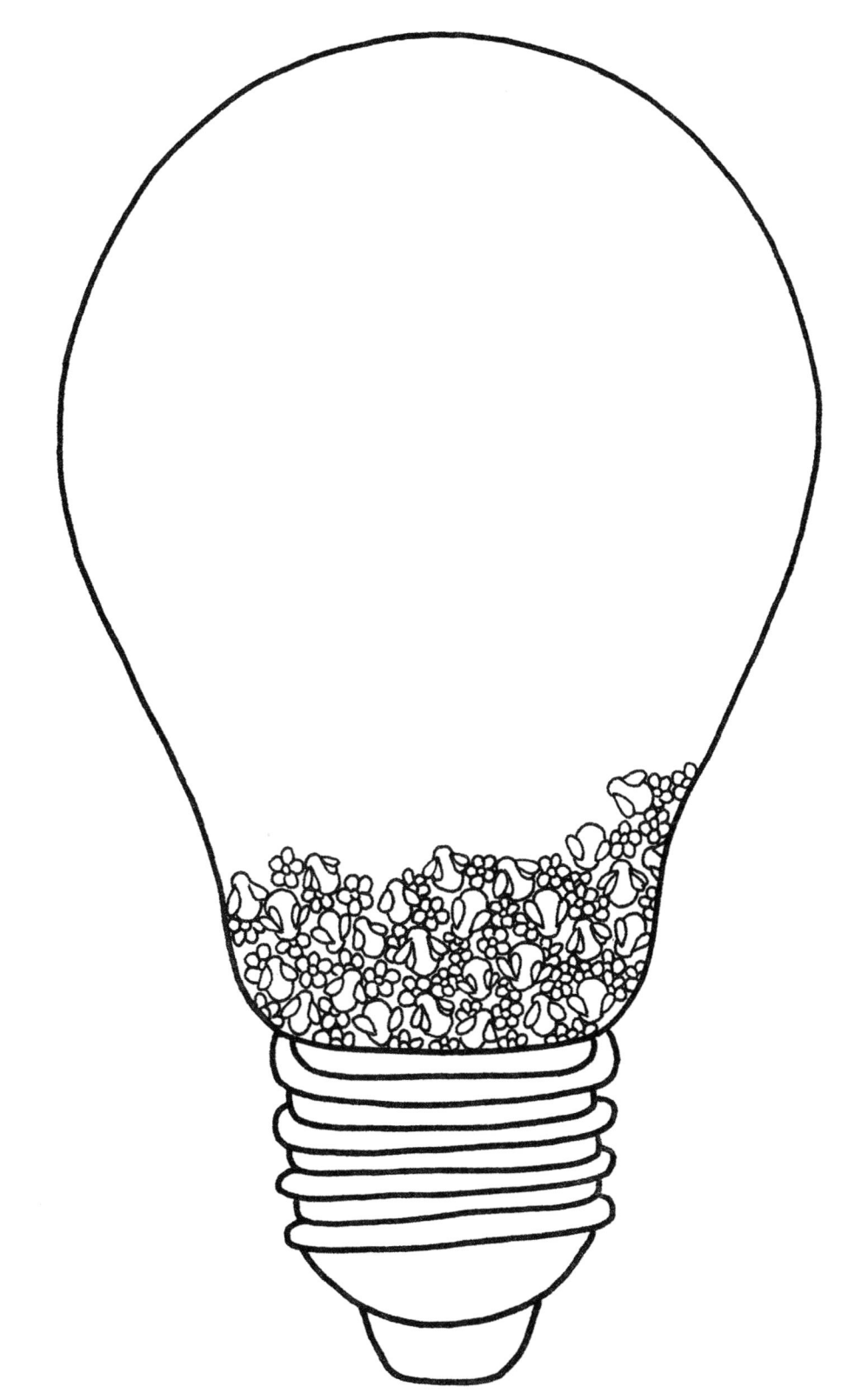

Tulip tree city

As a student, I had the opportunity to travel around Europe, thanks to the student exchange programs of European universities. During one such trip, I visited an arboretum in Slovakia—a magical place full of magnificent trees. I was incredibly impressed by the tulip tree and bought a seedling for my parents. It's been growing in their garden for over 20 years, but has not yet bloomed. For now I can only admire its majestic leaves.

In this drawing, I wanted to contrast the natural and the manmade, so I've used the tulip tree leaf as the frame and filled it with small houses. The content is therefore similar to that of the Tiny Houses Mandala (page 56), but here I've used a combination of color grading (as in the Spring Cat on page 28) and complementary colors. Try coloring the same drawing in different color schemes to see what effect this creates.

MATERIALS USED

- Fabriano 200gsm heavyweight paper
- Graphite pencil
- Staedtler 0.2mm black fineliner pen
- Faber-Castell Pitt Artist Pens (colors 107, 112, 113, 121, 162, 167, 170, 171, 172, 174, 219, 264)

Master the basics

Practice drawing some houses (shown in steps 1-4) on a separate sheet of paper.

Vary the height of the houses, the shapes of their windows, and the direction of the roof slope. As you add more houses around the first (shown in steps 1 and 2) try not to leave any spaces in between them.

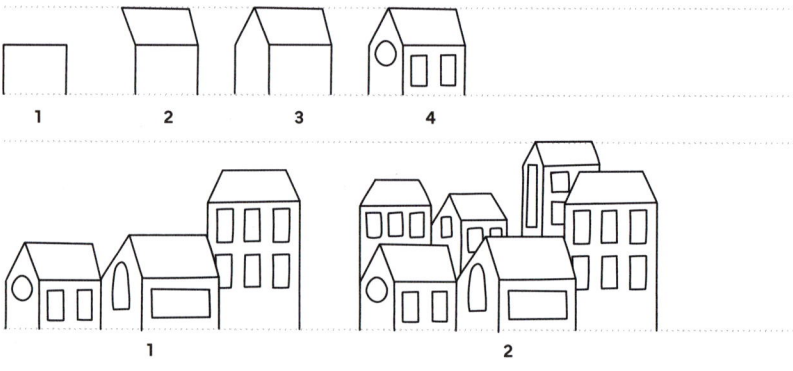

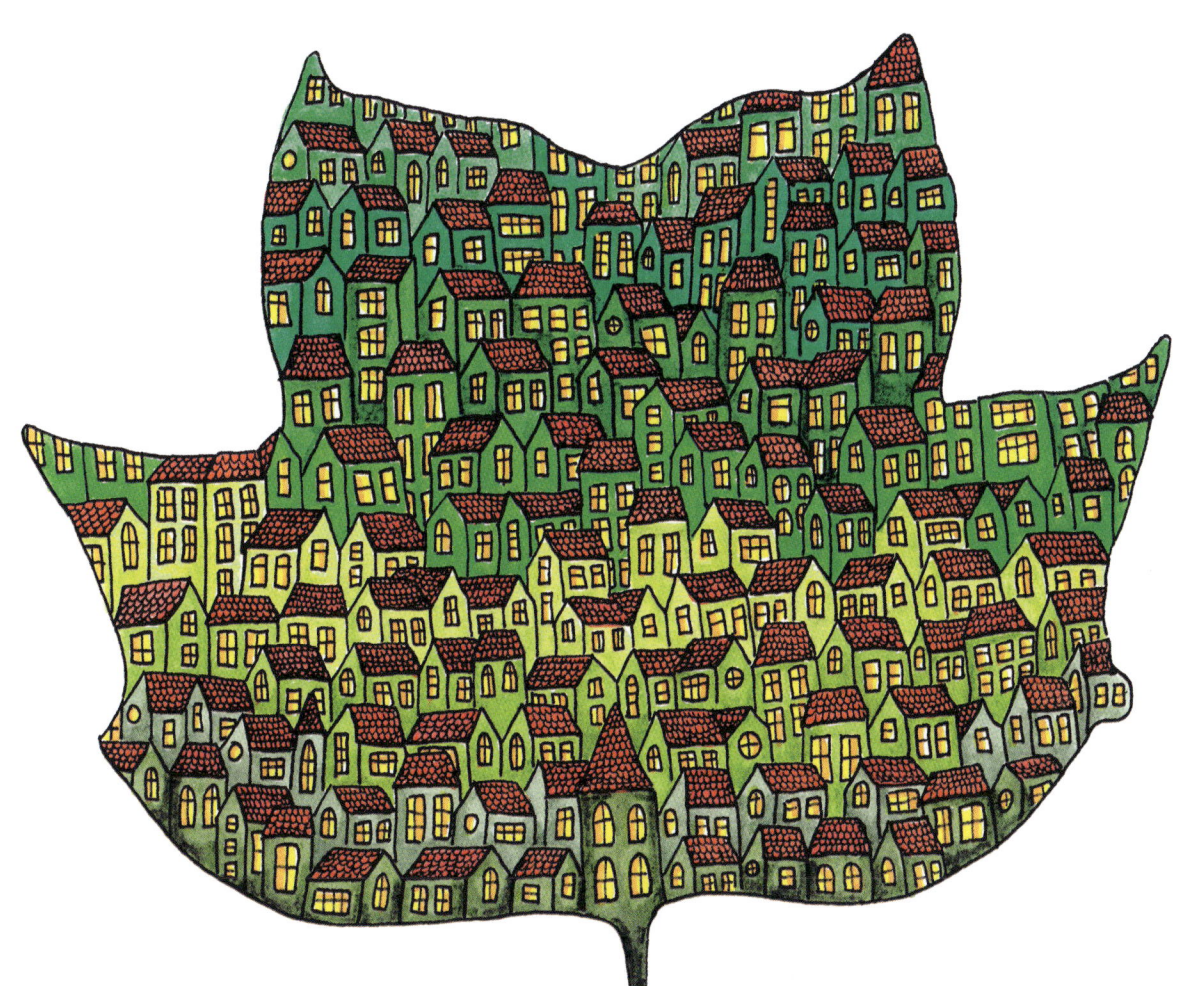

TIP Complementary colors are those that are opposite each other on a traditional artists' color wheel. Red is the complementary of green; orange is the complementary of blue; and purple is the complementary of yellow. When you add even a tiny amount of a complementary color to a drawing, it immediately makes it much more punchy and dynamic.

Drawing practice

How to draw and color key shapes

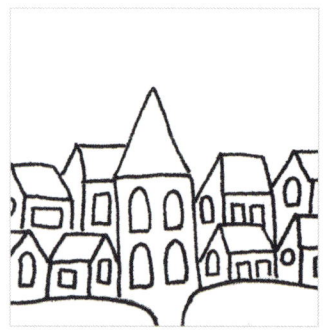

1 Start by drawing the leaf outline. Then draw the first row of houses at the base of the leaf. I decided to make my drawing fairly symmetrical, with a tall house at the tip of the stem and similar shapes and sizes on either side of it.

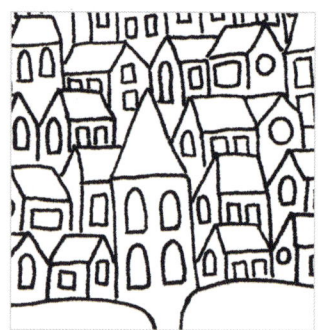

2 Add more rows of houses at different angles until you've filled the entire leaf. Go over the pencil lines with a black fineliner.

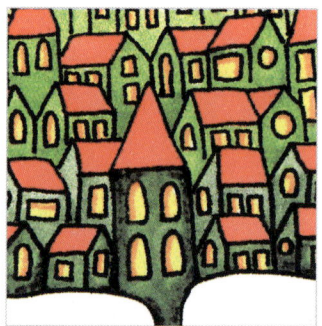

3 Now you can start coloring. I blocked in the roofs first, using a bright red. Next, color the facades. I used a complementary dark green for the stem and the first row of houses, then graded through more yellowy greens up to the middle of the leaf, before going back to darker, bluer greens for the top of the leaf.

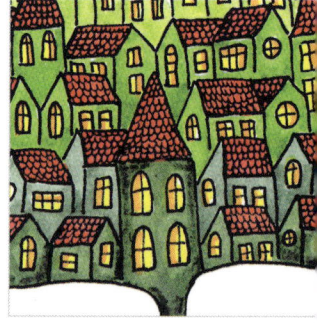

4 Finally, add the glazing bars to the bright windows and the individual roof tiles, using a black fineliner.

Practice here

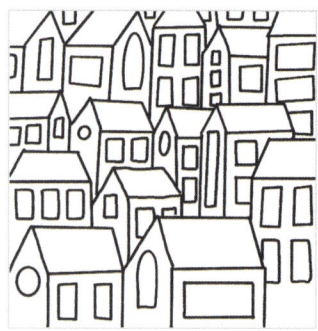

Practice color grading the buildings, adding roof details.

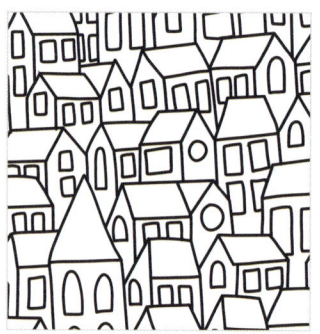

Add other details if you wish, such as snow on the rooftops or tiny figures in the windows.

Practice composition by drawing overlapping buildings in this box.

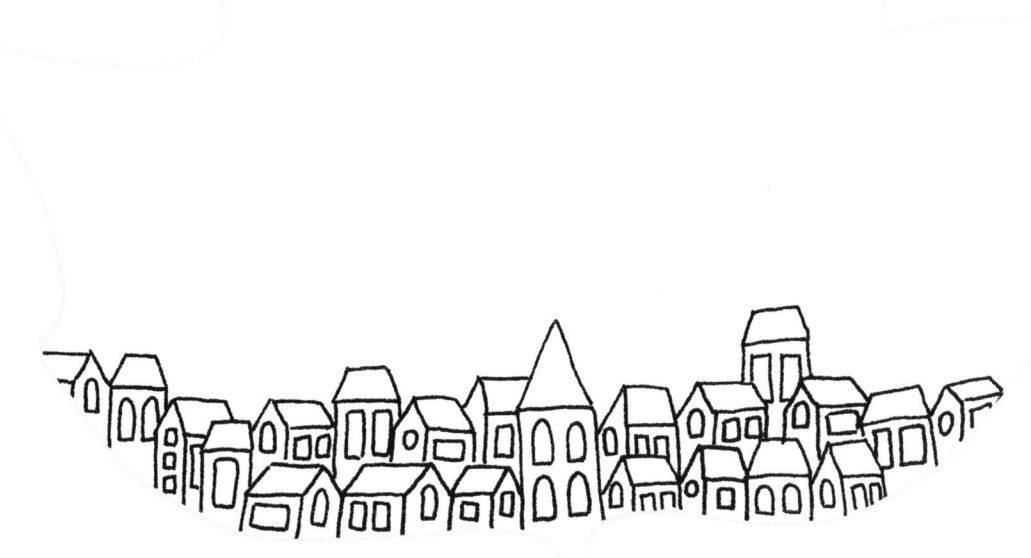

Tulip heart

The Netherlands is considered to be the country where tulips come from. However, nothing could be further from the truth: tulips were brought to the Netherlands only in 1562, on French ships sailing from Constantinople (now Istanbul) to Antwerp. From that moment on, the cultivation of tulips began. There are 120 species of tulips and at least 15,000 cultivated varieties.

Tulips are believed to symbolize love and signal the arrival of spring. Red tulips represent true love (hence the heart shape that I've chosen for this drawing), white tulips say, "I'm sorry," and purple tulips symbolize royal glory.

This drawing is an exercise in creating a sense of movement—just like tulip flowers dancing in the breeze. As you work your way up the shape, make a conscious effort to vary the angles of the stalks a little and to offset each set of the stalks from the ones below so that you don't end up with rigid vertical lines running through your drawing.

MATERIALS USED

- Fabriano 200gsm heavyweight paper
- Graphite pencil
- Staedtler 0.1mm black fineliner pen
- Faber-Castell Pitt Artist Pens (colors 112, 125, 129, 131, 133, 134, 136, 170, 172, 174, 223, 264)

Master the basics

Tulips are very sculptural and one of the simplest flowers to draw. Start with a small oval at a slight diagonal angle on the left (1), add a matching oval on the right (2), then draw the tip of an oval in between and a stalk below (3). A small leaf on either side of the stalk completes the shape (4).

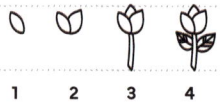

Try drawing individual tulips and tulip clusters on these practice lines.

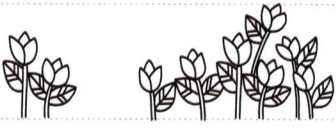

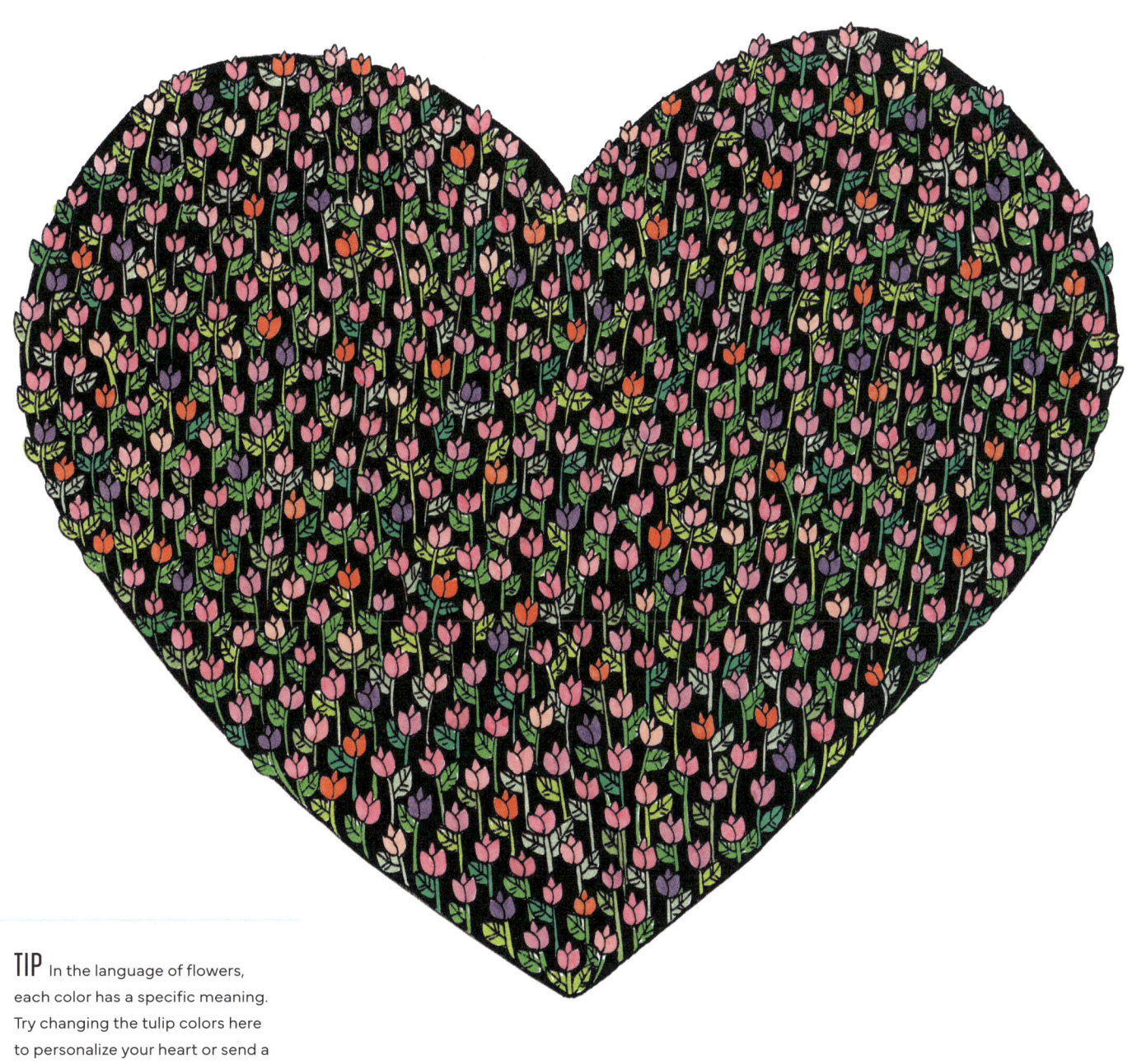

TIP In the language of flowers, each color has a specific meaning. Try changing the tulip colors here to personalize your heart or send a message through your drawing.

Drawing practice

How to draw and color key shapes

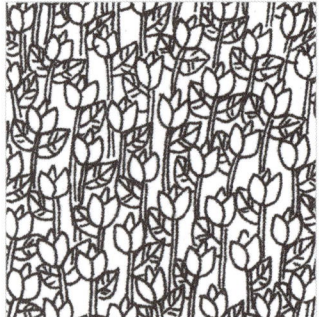

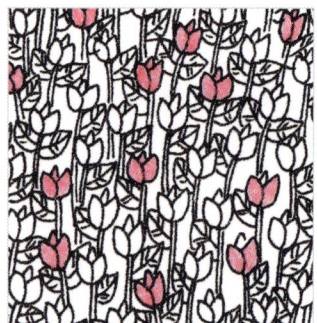

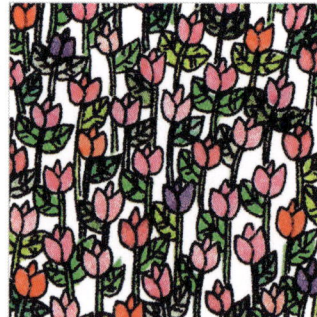

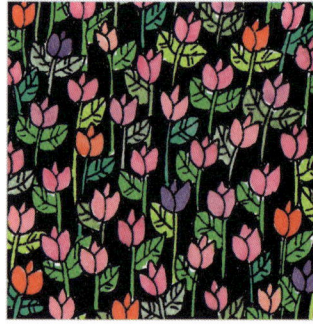

1 Start by drawing the heart outline. Begin filling it at the bottom and work your way up, curving some of the flower stalks a little and using the shapes of the leaves to get as close to the outline of the heart as you can.

2 Fill the entire shape with tulips. Although the stalks are long and thin, try to offset them from the ones below to avoid repetitive vertical rows. Then begin coloring the flowerheads in the color of your favorite tulip.

3 Use several colors (I chose mostly pinks and purples) for your tulips, then the drawing will not be so monochromatic. Use a range of greens, from a light yellowy green to a deeper sap green, for the leaves.

4 Leave the background until last. You can color it or leave it white—choose what you like best.

Practice here

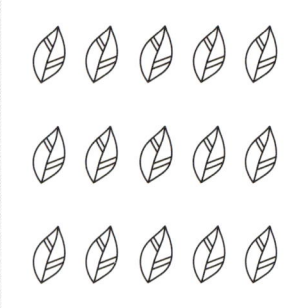

Practice your leaf color palette above.

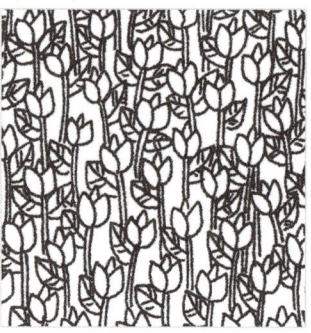

Color in these tulips and leaves.

Try filling in from scratch in this outline.

TIP The leaves may seem like secondary elements in this drawing, but they can still be just as interesting as the flowers! Varying the shades of green you use for the leaves will make your drawing more dynamic.

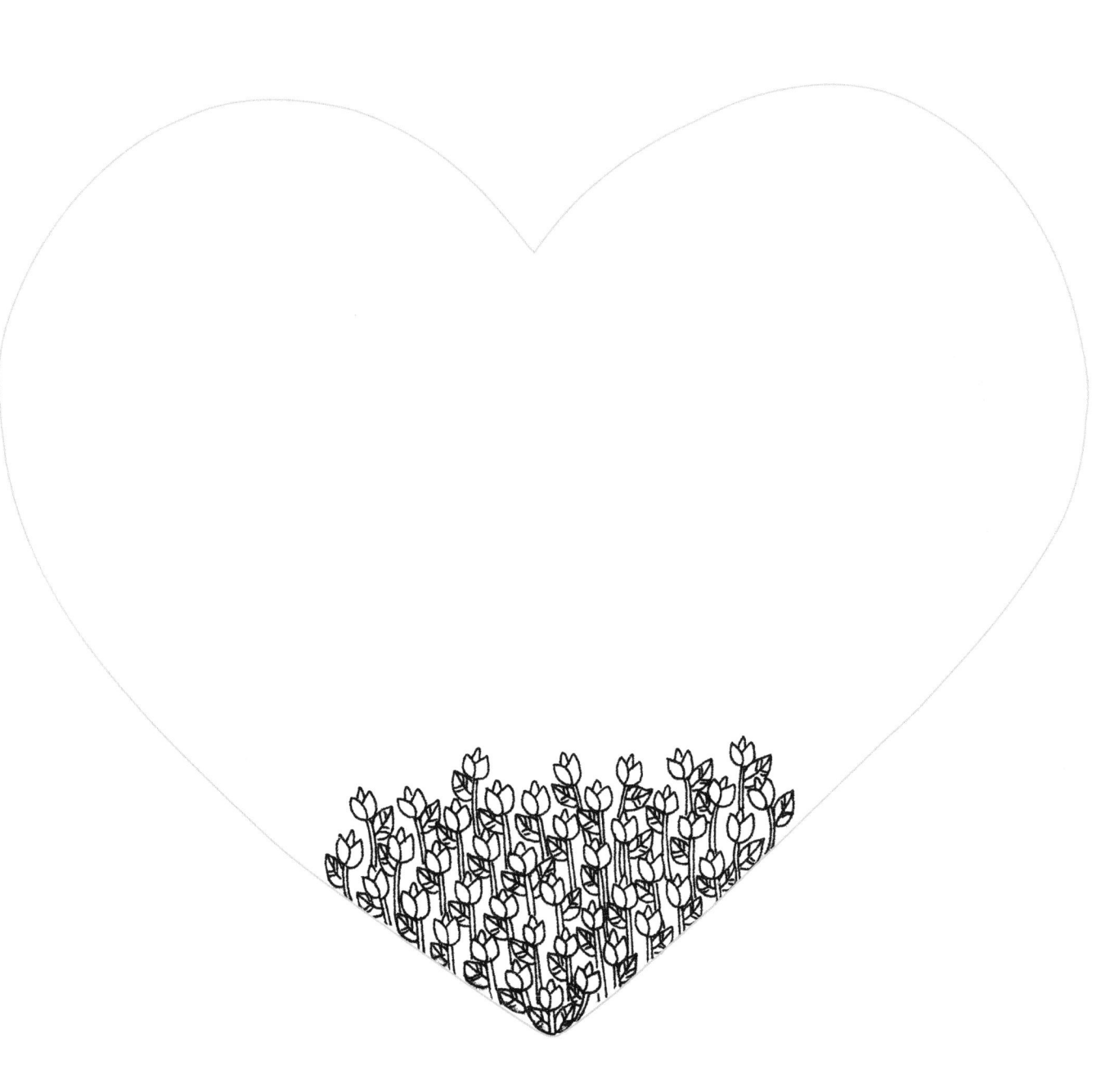

Moon cats

Cats are considered among the most magical of animals. In ancient Egypt they were believed to be sacred; in Norse mythology they accompanied the goddess Freya; and in the Middle Ages they were seen as the companions and familiars of witches. Although they might appear to be somewhat aloof and inscrutable, any cat lover will tell you that they have very different personalities and moods—and that's what I wanted to convey in this drawing. Cats are nocturnal animals and, like the moon, are active at night. This is why you can often find a combination of a cat and the moon in art, so a crescent moon seemed like the perfect shape to use here.

MATERIALS USED

- Fabriano 200gsm heavyweight paper
- Graphite pencil
- Staedtler 0.1mm black fineliner pen
- Faber-Castell Pitt Artist Pens (colors 104, 107, 109, 113, 116, 131, 132, 189, 268, 272)

Master the basics

My cats all follow the same basic outline, but by altering the shape of the eyes or the size of the pupils you can give them a range of expressions, from flirtatious to sleepy to grumpy and much more!

Look at cartoons or photos of cats to see how many different expressions you can pick out, then try transferring those expressions to paper. You may also practice drawing your cats in the blank spaces on these lines.

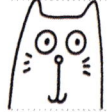

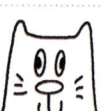

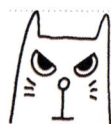

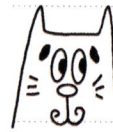

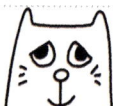

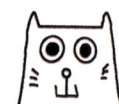

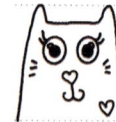

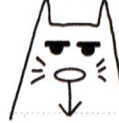

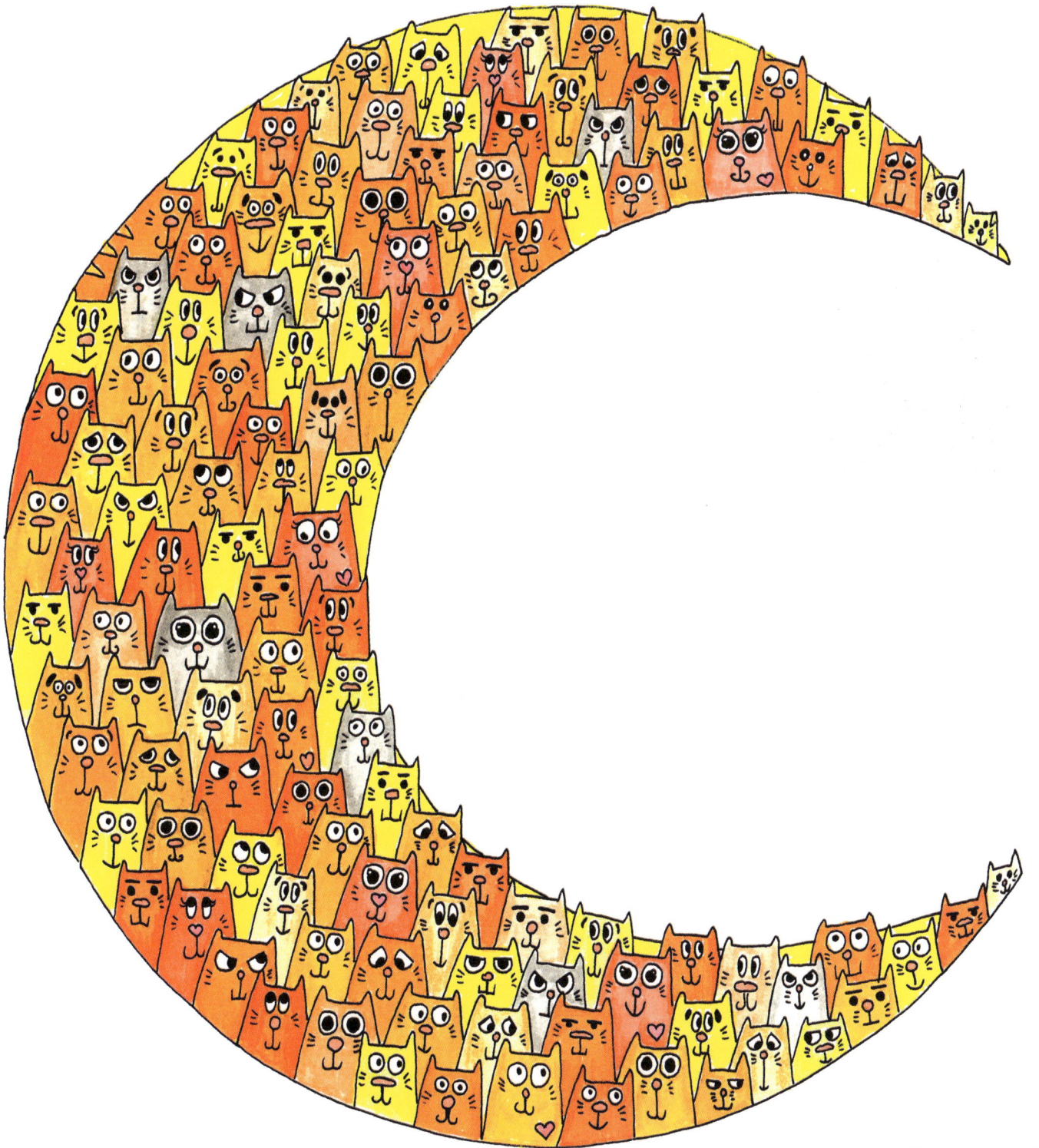

Drawing practice

How to draw and color key shapes

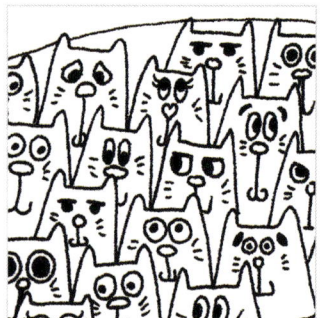

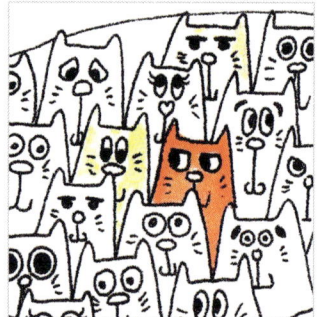

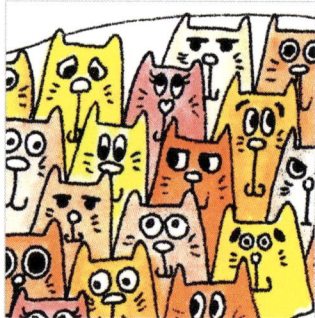

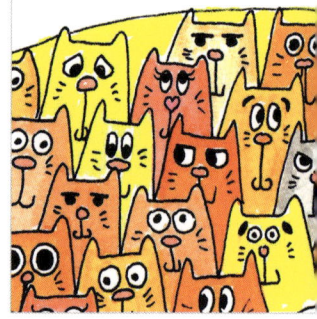

1 Start by drawing the moon outline. Draw cats along the bottom edge of the moon, then add cats behind them on a slight diagonal. On the inside curve of the crescent, allow the cats' ears to stick up a tiny bit above the outline.

2 Continue until you've filled the entire shape, then go over the pencil lines with a black fineliner. Begin coloring with your first two colors, remembering to leave the pupils of the eyes and the noses white.

3 I chose warm colors—yellow, orange, pink, and red—for my cats and even left a few cats white for variety. However, remember that our cats are mythical creatures, so they can be any color you like—blue, green, red, or even a regal purple.

4 My cats are closely packed together, but in the final stage I filled in the few gaps that were left with a vivid yellow which is not only a lively, vibrant color but also makes me think of the light of the moon shining down on us.

Practice here

Draw a cat from scratch, adding an expression of your choice.

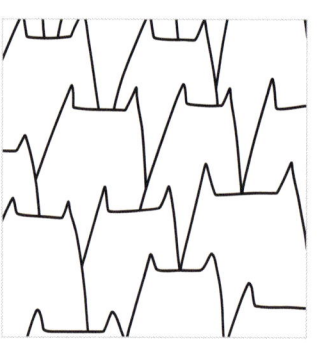

Fill these cat outlines with faces.

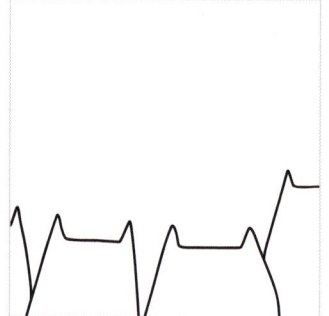

Complete the cat pattern, adding faces as you go.

TIPS If you often use this crescent moon shape for drawings, create a template for yourself to make it easier and faster to replicate.

Practice drawing your cats' expressions on a separate sheet of paper first. If you are not sure of your abilities, use a graphite pencil. This will make it easier to change your drawing if you make mistakes.

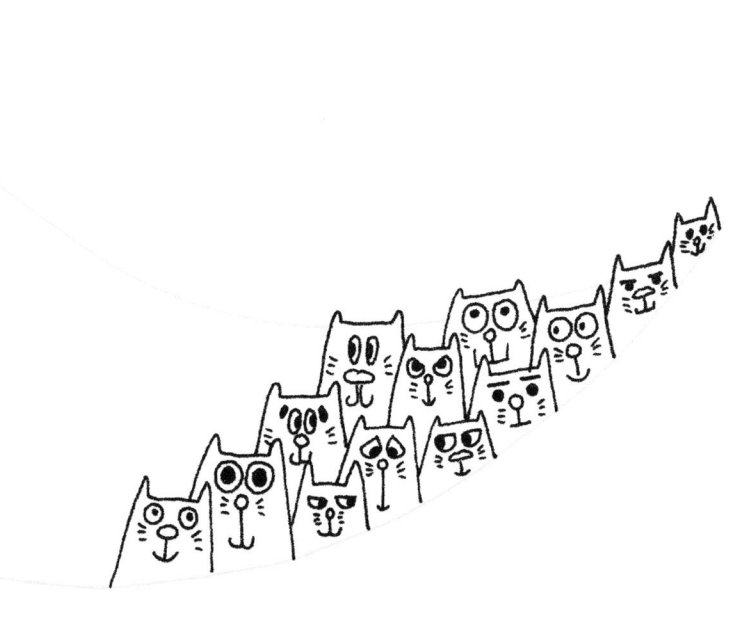

Ladybug heart

Did you know that the ladybug is a symbol of a flower meadow, happiness, true love, and innocence? In Polish culture, a ladybug is considered a guest from heaven who, when returning, can take our wishes there. Traces of these beliefs remain not only in the Polish culture, in which the ladybug is also called "God's cow," but also in Germany, where it is called *Marienkaefer* (Mary's beetle). In France it is known as *bête à Bon Dieu* (a creation of the Good God). When you see a ladybug, think of your wish and send it out into the universe with gratitude and thanks!

MATERIALS USED

- Fabriano 200gsm heavyweight paper
- Graphite pencil
- Staedtler 0.2mm black fineliner pen
- Faber-Castell Pitt Artist Pens (colors 107, 110, 113, 118, 120, 121, 146, 219)

Master the basics

I've drawn my ladybugs from directly overhead, so the shapes are really simple. Start by drawing an oval for the body (1), add a crescent shape for the head (2), put in a dividing line down the center of the body (3), and finally add the dots (4).

Once you've drawn one ladybug, try drawing several close together on the blank practice line, following steps 1–3. Add flowers in between each ladybug.

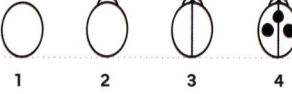

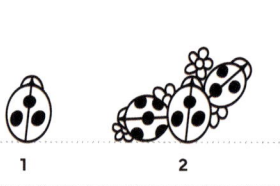
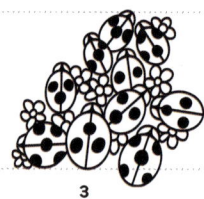

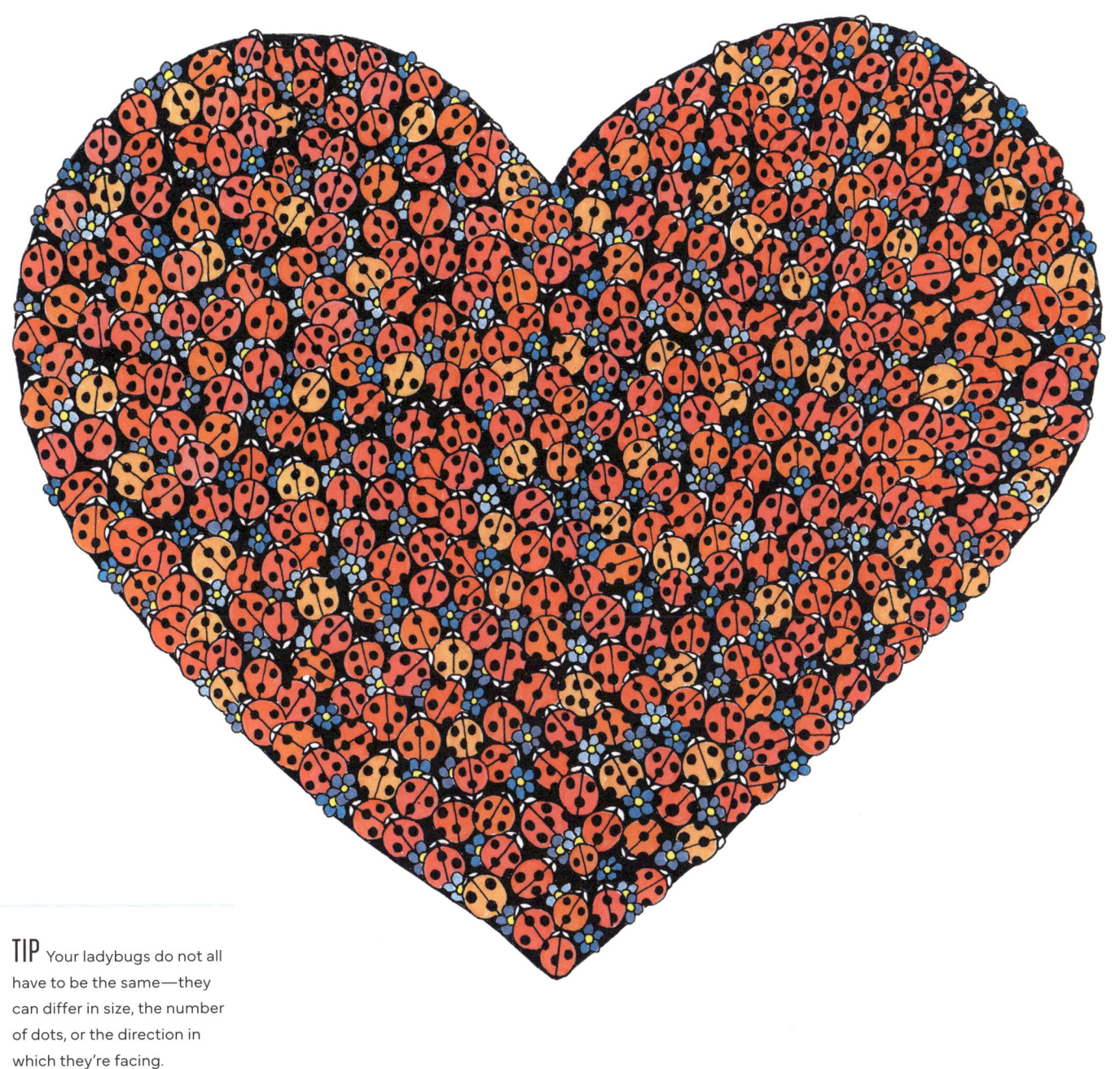

TIP Your ladybugs do not all have to be the same—they can differ in size, the number of dots, or the direction in which they're facing.

Drawing practice

How to draw and color key shapes

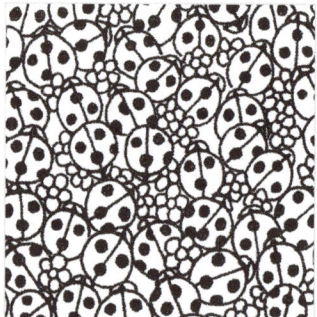

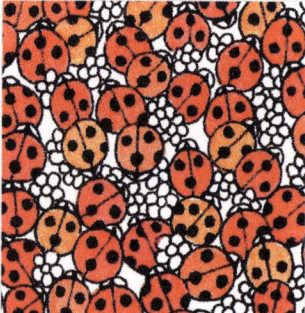

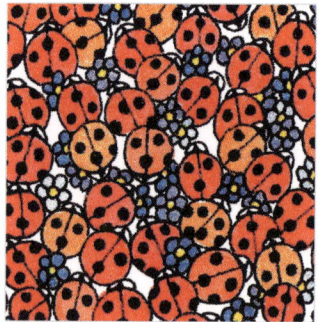

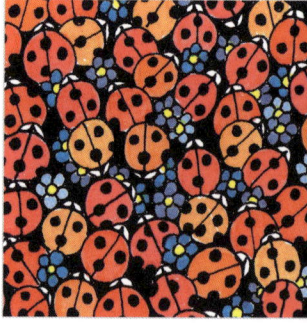

1 Start with drawing the heart outline. Then draw the ladybugs, working upward from the bottom of the heart. Vary the direction and number of dots as you go and overlap some ladybugs on others. Add flowers in between them.

2 When you've filled the heart with ladybugs and flowers, you can start coloring. Choose the colors you like the most. It can be a full palette of red, a bit of orange, or even yellow. Then move on to lighter reds and oranges.

3 Next, color the flowers. The flower color should contrast with the color of the ladybugs, so I opted for various shades of forget-me-not blue.

4 Finally, fill the background with the color of your choice

Practice here

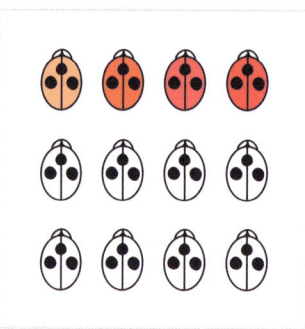

Choose your color palette.

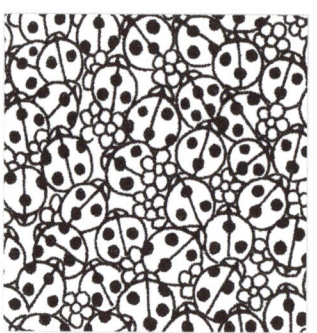

Color in the flowers and ladybugs, spreading out your chosen colors.

Try from scratch, filling this outline shape.

TIP Practice drawing the ladybugs on a separate sheet of drawing paper. To make it easier to change the direction of the ladybugs, just rotate your paper.

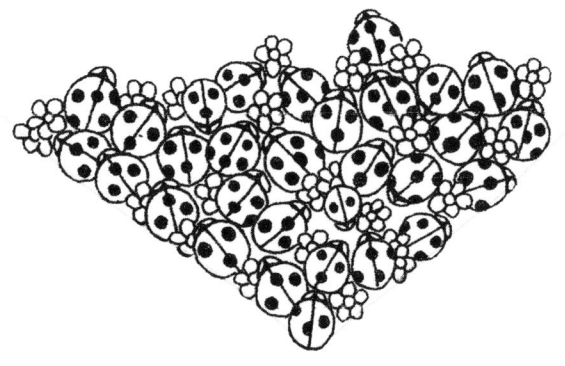

Leafy dog

This time, something for dog lovers! Although I'm a cat lover myself, I know dogs have a special meaning for many people. Just like my cat, dogs are also members of their humans' families. This drawing was created in honor of our four-legged friends, for their courage, for warmth, for friendship, for closeness, for love, for perseverance, for laughter, and for life!

   A side profile works best for the outline, as it shows the distinctive shape of each breed of dog's head. I chose to fill it with various types of leaves as a symbol of the diverse beauty of the natural world and the perfect harmony that exists between animals and nature.

MATERIALS USED

- Fabriano 200gsm heavyweight paper
- Graphite pencil
- Staedtler 0.1mm black fineliner pen
- Faber-Castell Pitt Artist Pens (colors 109, 112, 113, 154, 161, 162, 167, 170, 172, 174, 264, 268)

Master the basics

Here are some of the leaves I put in my drawing, but you can also invent your own. Whatever kind of leaves you choose to draw, aim for a good variety of shapes—elongated, rounded, irregular shapes like oak or holly leaves, or leaves arranged symmetrically on either side of a central stem, work particularly well.

Use the blank space on these lines to practice drawing these various leaf shapes, or to create your own.

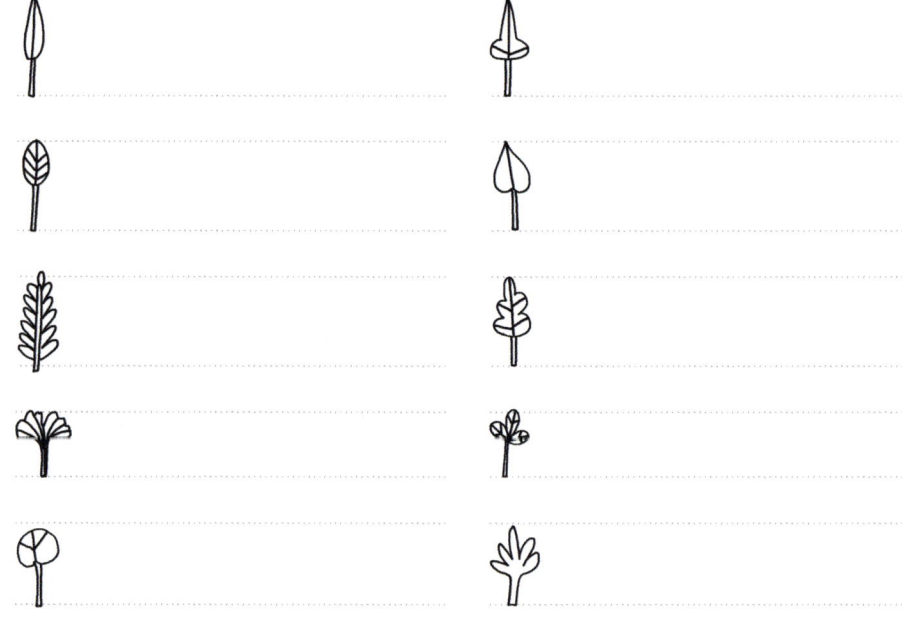

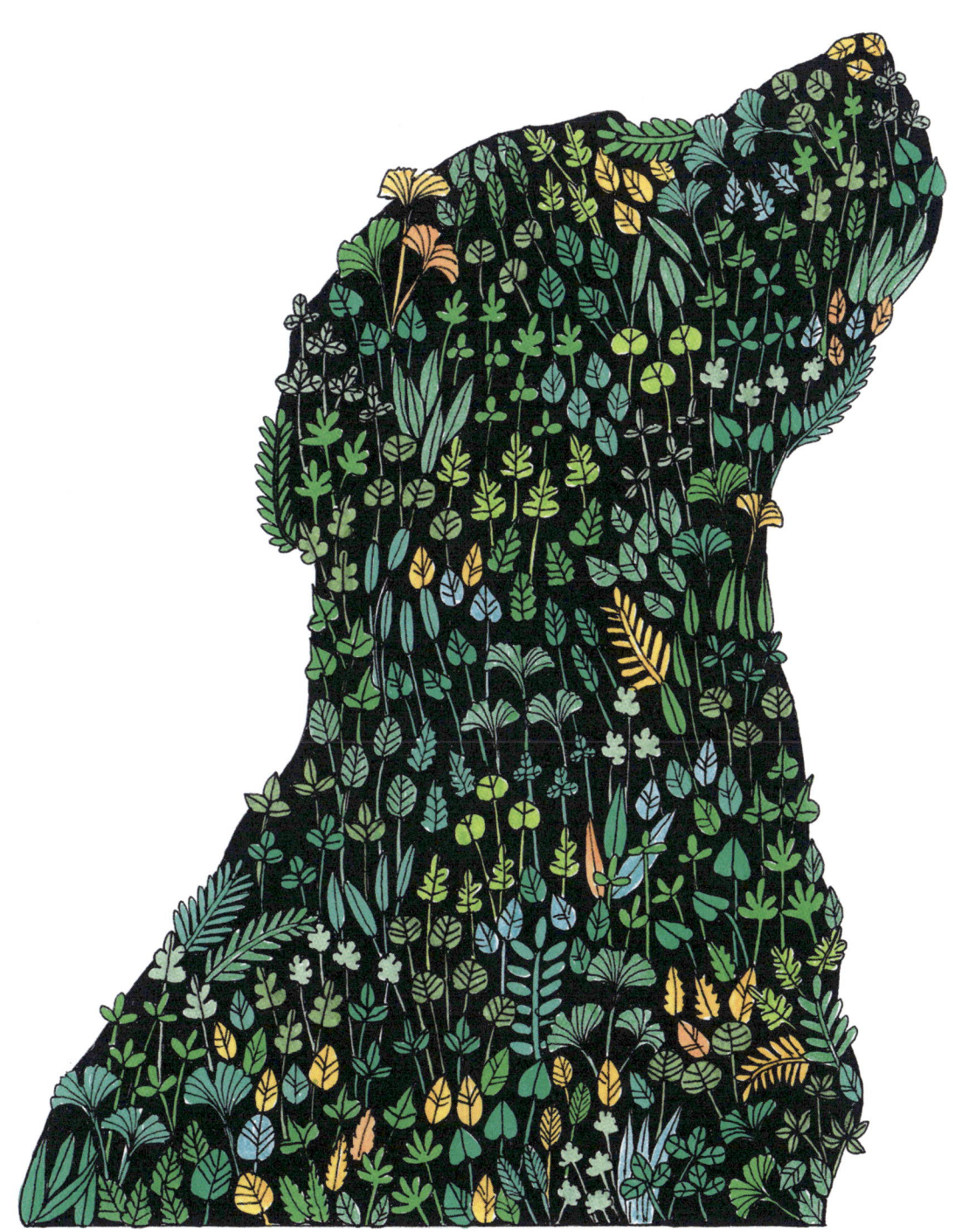

Drawing practice

How to draw and color key shapes

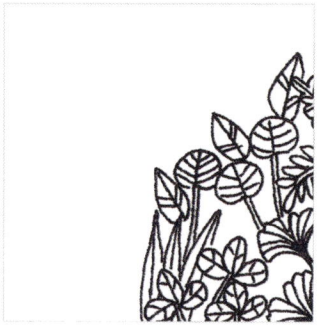 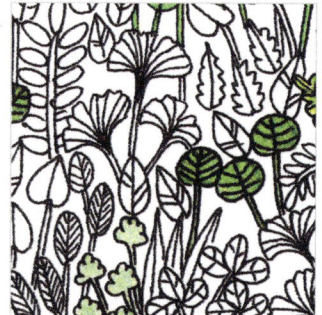 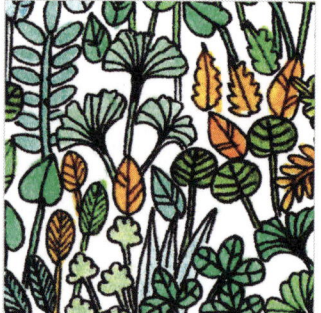 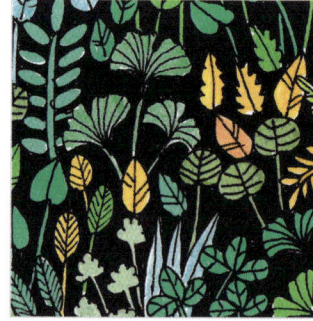

1 Start with drawing the dog outline, then fill it with leaves, starting in the bottom corner. You can use the examples I've provided or create your own unique patterns. I like to group small clusters of similar-shaped leaves together, to provide some visual continuity.

2 Fill the shape. I like to have a few very small leaves sticking out beyond the silhouette itself, as this looks like wispy bits of fur. Go over the pencil lines with a black fineliner, then begin coloring. Work with one color at a time, filling in all of one type of leaf before moving on to the next.

3 Introduce some contrasting colors as you go—oranges and blue-greens, for example—to add variety.

4 As always, leave the background until the end. You can color it black like I did or leave it blank if you prefer.

Practice here

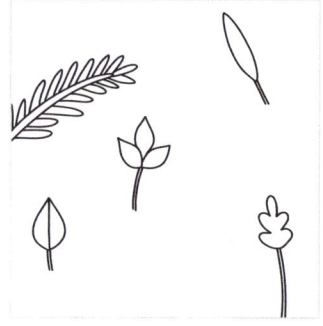  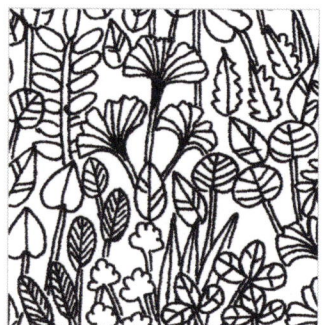

Turn these individual leaves into clusters, remembering to add details.

Fill this outline with leaves.

Color the elements in this box.

TIP For the leaves, you can choose whichever color palette you like, from greens and yellows to browns and oranges. Match the colors to your favorite season.

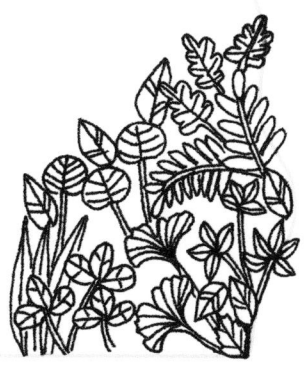

Tiny houses mandala

I like to make a connection between the shape my drawings are contained in and the subjects that fill them. A simple circle reminds me of the Earth as seen from space, and I wanted to draw something relating to the impact that humankind has had on our crowded planet. I didn't forget about the natural world, but I wanted to present a slightly different view so I chose to fill my circle with tiny houses and skyscrapers.

In this drawing, tall skyscrapers tower above smaller, more humble dwellings, so as you work you'll need to keep stepping back and viewing it as a whole to keep everything looking balanced. What ties it all together is the repetition of simple geometric shapes—rectangles and squares for the buildings, doors, and windows, and triangles for the pitched roofs.

MATERIALS USED

- Fabriano 200gsm heavyweight paper
- Graphite pencil
- Compass or small plate to draw around
- Staedtler 0.2mm black fineliner pen
- Faber-Castell Pitt Artist Pens (colors 104, 107, 109, 113, 114, 116, 131, 132, 148, 179, 189, 192, 220, 239, 270, 272)

Master the basics

Here are some examples of the buildings I placed in the drawing. However, don't be afraid to create your own shapes—the best advice I can give to artists, both beginners and professionals, is to let your imagination run wild!

Experiment with your own building styles on a separate sheet of paper.

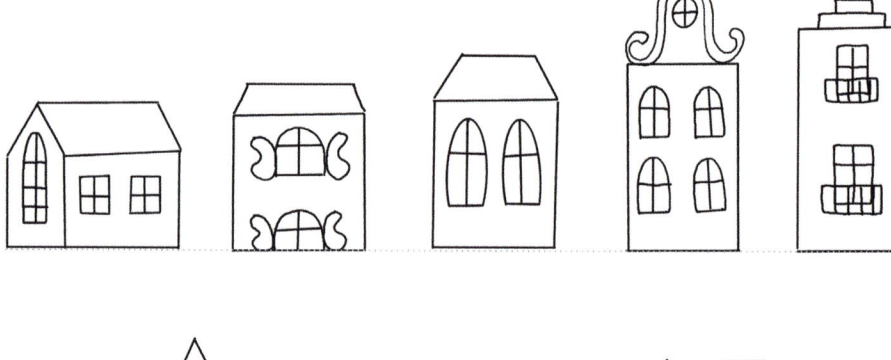

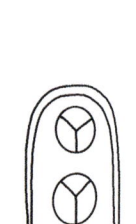 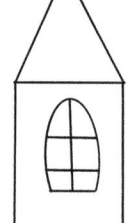 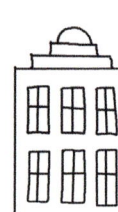 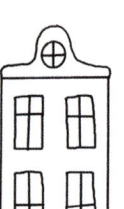 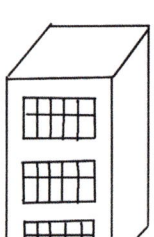 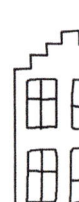

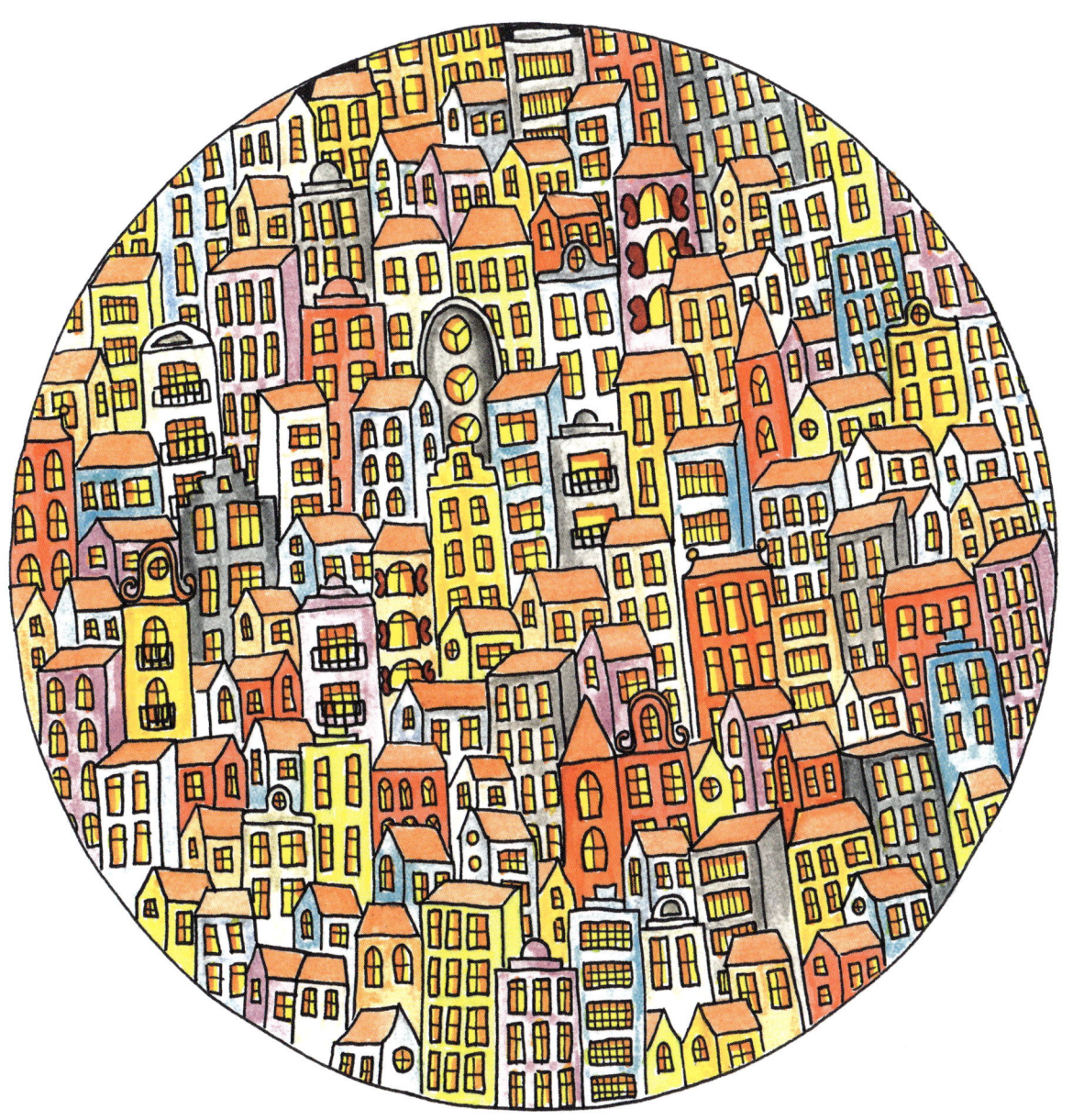

Drawing practice

How to draw and color key shapes

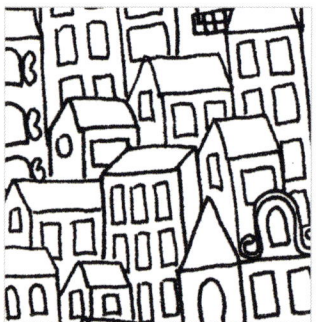 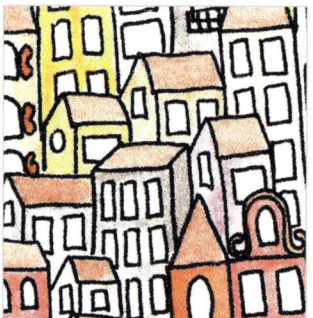 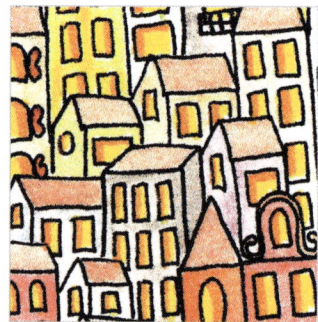 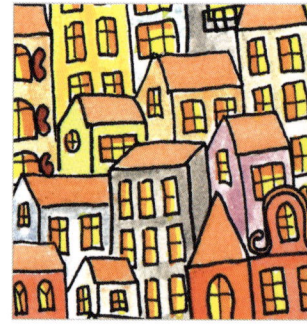

1 Start with using the compass to draw the circle. Working from the bottom up, using a graphite pencil then a black fineliner pen, begin filling the circle with rows of small houses. Keep to simple shapes and allow some of the houses to overlap.

2 Once your circle is full, you can start coloring. Block in the colors of the walls first, leaving the doors and windows white.

3 Continue coloring, using whatever colors take your fancy. Begin blocking in the roofs, too—but leave some buildings white so as not to overpower the drawing.

4 Add window details at the very end. Use two colors: a primary color such as red for one half of the window and a secondary color such as orange for the other. This creates the illusion of light in the windows.

Practice here

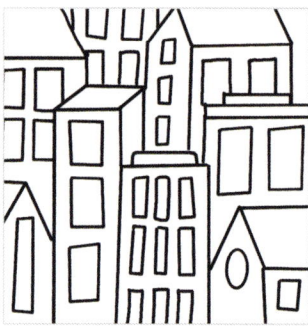 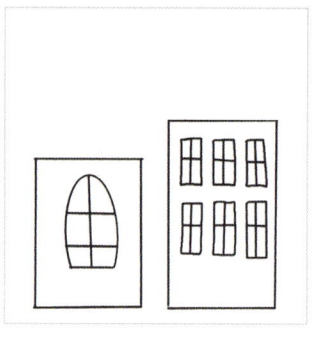 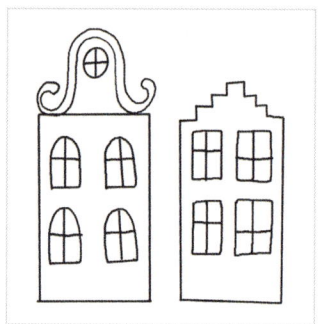

Practice coloring these houses.

Add roofs to these houses.

Experiment with details here by adding extra features to these buildings.

TIP The buildings should differ in size, number of windows, and shape. You can present either a front or a side view. I opted for warm colors—yellows, oranges, and reds—to give my drawing some tonal consistency. These are also the colors of brick and sandstone, from which many buildings are made.

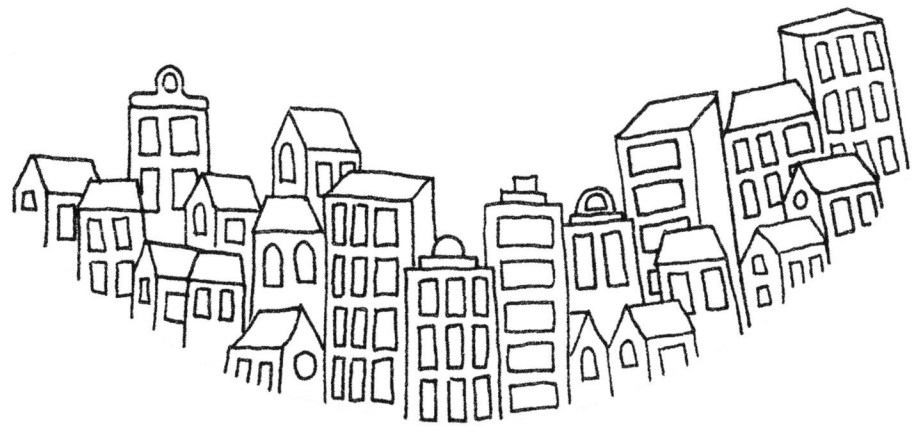

Rubber duckies

Who among us hasn't had or doesn't have a rubber duck? They accompanied us in water fun, either at home or in the pool. Rubber ducks remain extremely popular to this day. You can even visit a museum of rubber ducks—there's one in Amsterdam, the Netherlands, and another in Bydgoszcz, Poland.

See just how imaginative you can be in giving your ducks different personalities. Just by altering the eyes, you can make them look coy or cunning, goofy or gorgeous. You can vary their accessories by playing around with hats, ties, or cool shades. You can even add some decorative details, such as flowers or hearts. There's a rubber duck for every mood!

MATERIALS USED

- Fabriano 200gsm heavyweight paper
- Graphite pencil
- Compass or small plate to draw around
- Staedtler 0.1mm black fineliner pen
- Faber-Castell Pitt Artist Pens (colors 107, 108, 109, 112, 113, 120, 129, 134, 146, 153, 186, 219, 268, 272)

Master the basics

Draw an incomplete oval shape for the duck's head and body, then play around with the features. The pupils of the eyes can be round or semi-circular, positioned centrally or to one side; the beak can be drawn straight on or slightly angled; you can choose whether or not to add eyebrows and eyelashes—all these variations give your ducks their individual characters.

Accessories—a pirate's hat, some devil's horns, a flowery fascinator, for example—express the ducks' personalities, too. Here are some ideas to get you started.

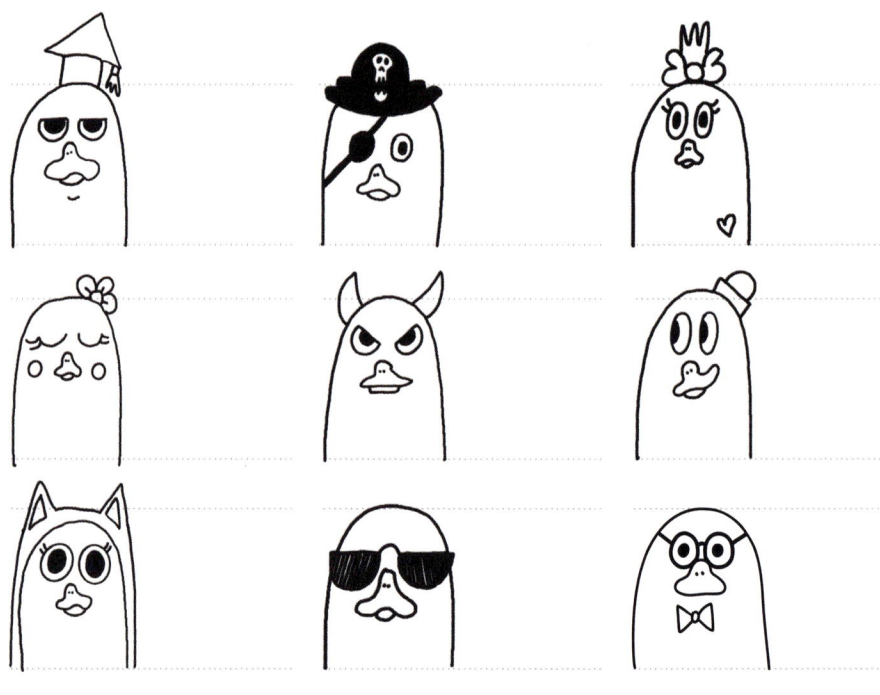

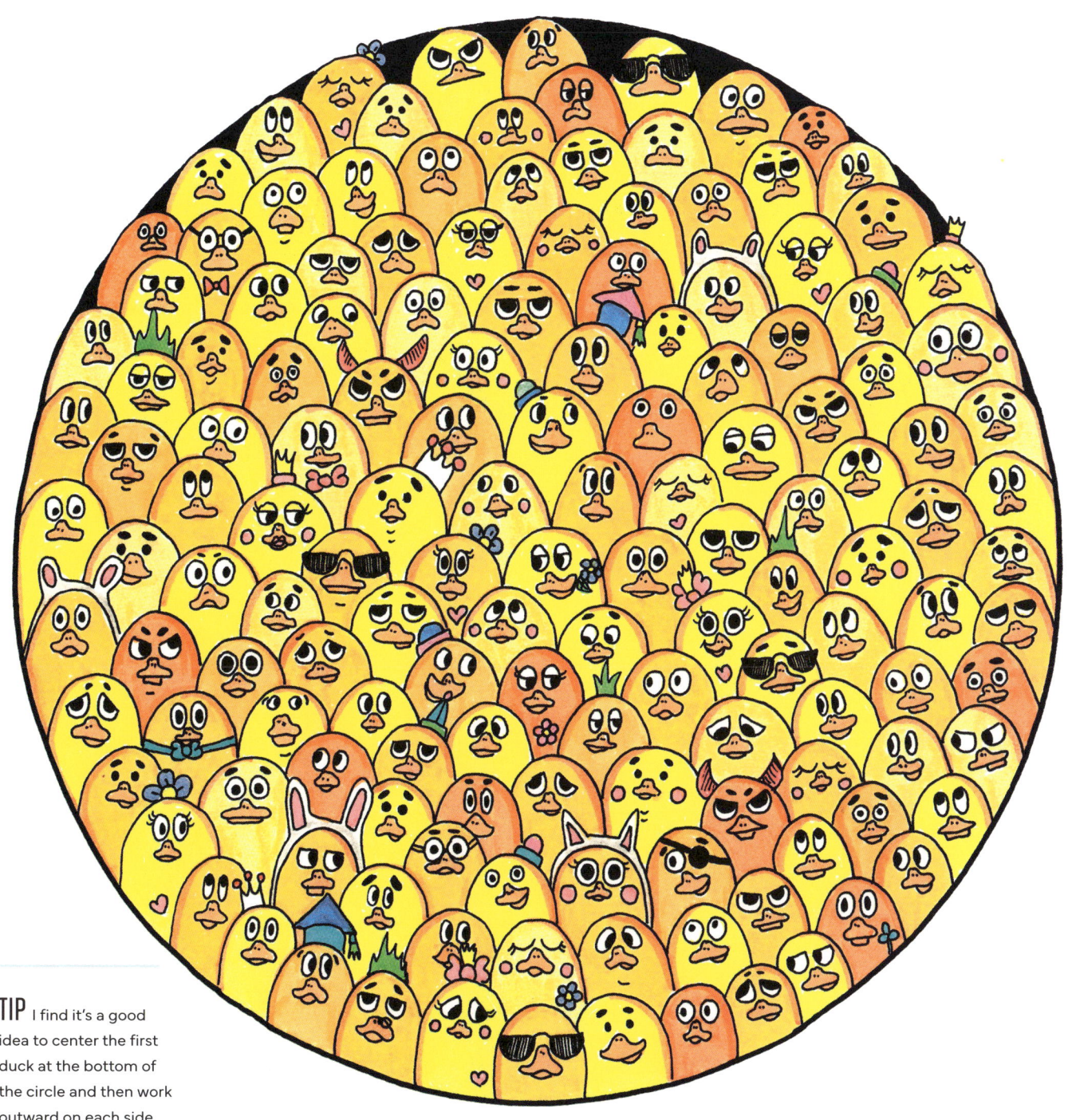

Drawing practice

How to draw and color key shapes

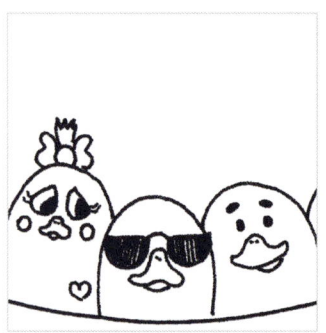

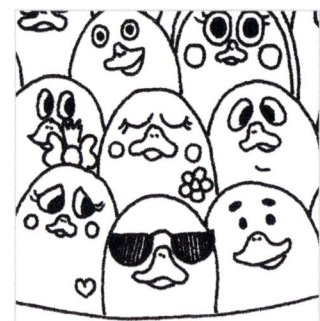

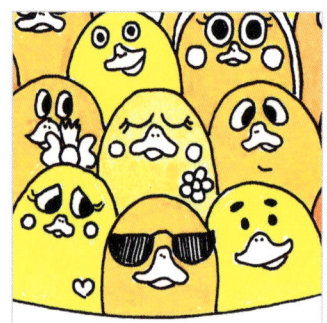

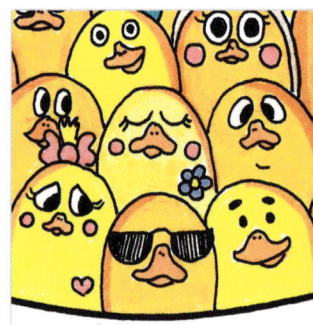

1 Start with using your compass to draw the circle. Begin filling the circle with ducks at the bottom and work your way up.

2 When you've got three or four ducks on each side of the first central one, start adding more ducks behind, slightly offsetting the ducks from row to row. I packed my ducks tightly together, leaving only a few blank spaces at the top of the circle.

3 Once you have drawn all the ducks, start coloring. First, color the ducks themselves, leaving the beaks and accessories blank for now. I chose a palette of yellow, orange, and brown, but you can use completely different colors because, as we all know, rubber ducks can be any color.

4 Color the beaks (making sure they stand out colorwise from the ducks' heads) and accessories. Finally fill in any gaps between the ducks; in my drawing, this was just a few tiny spaces at the very top.

Practice here

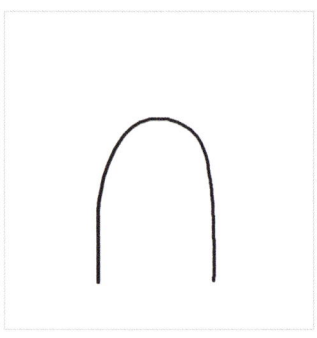

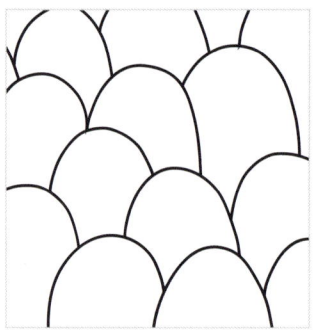

Design your own duck character in this box.

Add faces and accessories to these outlines.

Fill this shape with ducks.

TIP Think carefully about how you're going to make each duck different from its neighbor. Experiment on scrap paper before you begin your actual drawing.

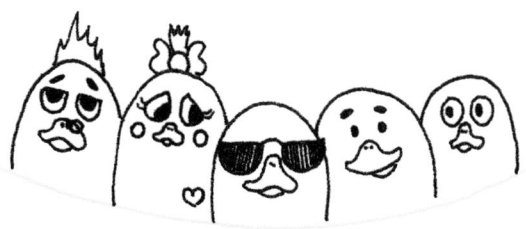

Mushroom moon

The moon accompanies us every night, illuminating the corners of a dark room or guiding us during evening walks. There is nothing more pleasant than watching the starry sky on a warm night while lying on a blanket spread over grass—this is one of my favorite summer memories.

The moon is magical, and magic has its own rules, so let's introduce some of our own unique magic into this fairytale drawing! Give your imagination free rein by not only creating new mushrooms to fill your moon, but also using unusual colors. Who said that mushrooms cannot be blue, yellow, purple, or pink? Indulge your creativity—there are no rules here!

MATERIALS USED

- Fabriano 200gsm heavyweight paper
- Graphite pencil
- Staedtler 0.1mm black fineliner pen
- Faber-Castell Pitt Artist Pens (colors 107, 109, 112, 113, 121, 133, 146, 156, 162, 170, 192, 219, 232, 264, 268)

Master the basics

Here are some basic mushroom shapes for you to copy or interpret in your own way. Follow the step-by-step guide for the top two mushrooms, then practice drawing the others on the blank lines.

Note how I've varied the shape (some are rounded, some are popsicle shaped, and some are triangular), viewpoint (you can see the gills on the underside of some fungi), and height of the mushrooms.

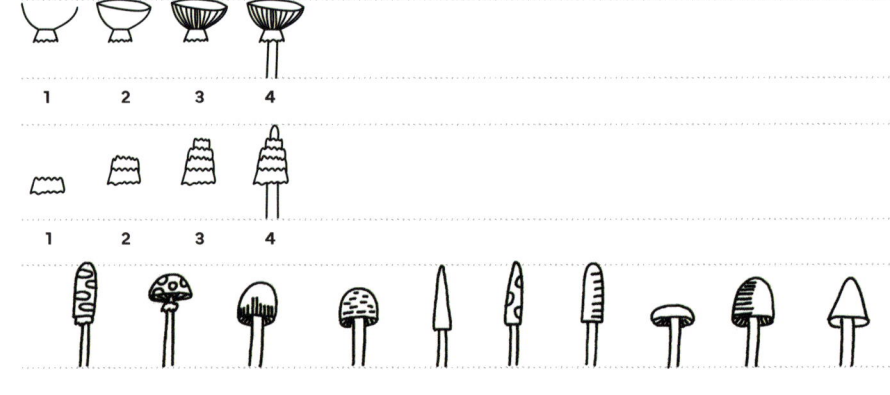

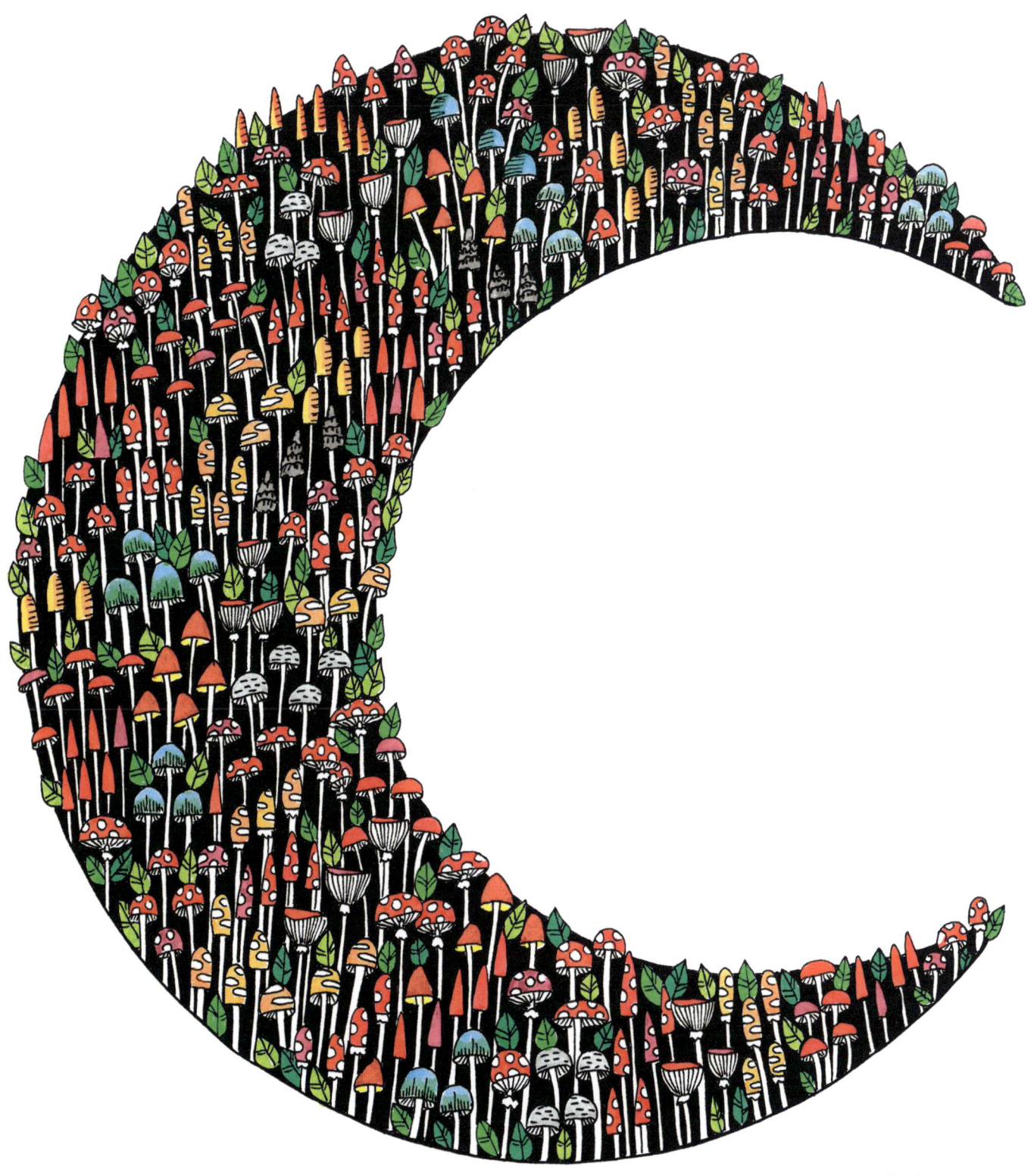

Drawing practice

How to draw and color key shapes

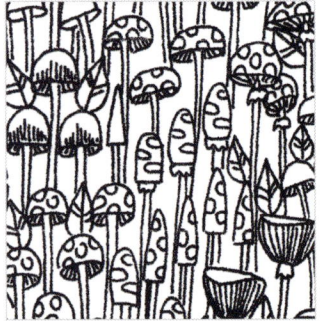

1 Start with using the compass to draw your crescent moon outline. Using a graphite pencil then a black fineliner, begin filling your moon with different types of mushrooms. Add some leaves in between the mushrooms.

2 Continue until you've filled the moon completely, making sure you vary the height, size, and shape of your mushrooms. Add little dots to some for that classic fairytale feel! Once you've filled your shape, start coloring, but leave the stalks and gills white.

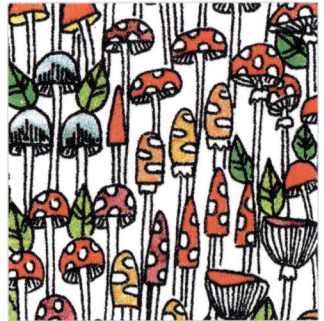

3 Move on to your next group of colors. Add a few horizontal strokes in black fineliner or a darker tone of your main color to the right-hand side of some mushrooms to make them look more three-dimensional.

4 Once you've colored everything in, add the black background.

Practice here

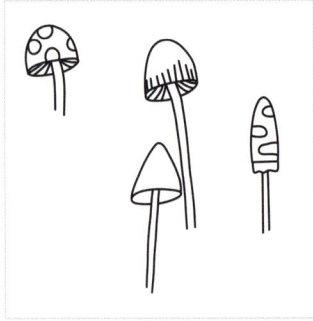

Fill in mushroom clusters, grouping three or four of the same mushroom together.

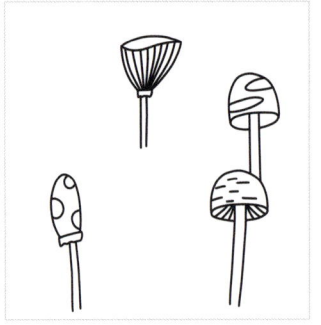

Fill in mushroom clusters with these variations. Don't forget to add leaves!

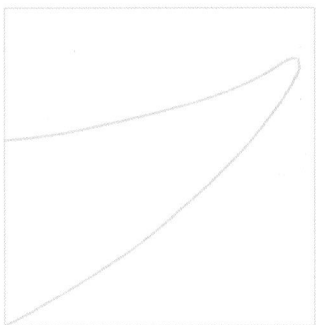

Try from scratch inside this outline.

TIP The placement of the mushrooms isn't completely random here: I find that grouping little clusters of the same kind of mushroom together, just as they would grow in the wild, creates a more naturalistic feel. To get a good color balance, put in your main colors one at a time—so all the reds, then all the yellows and oranges, and so on—distributing them fairly evenly across the drawing.

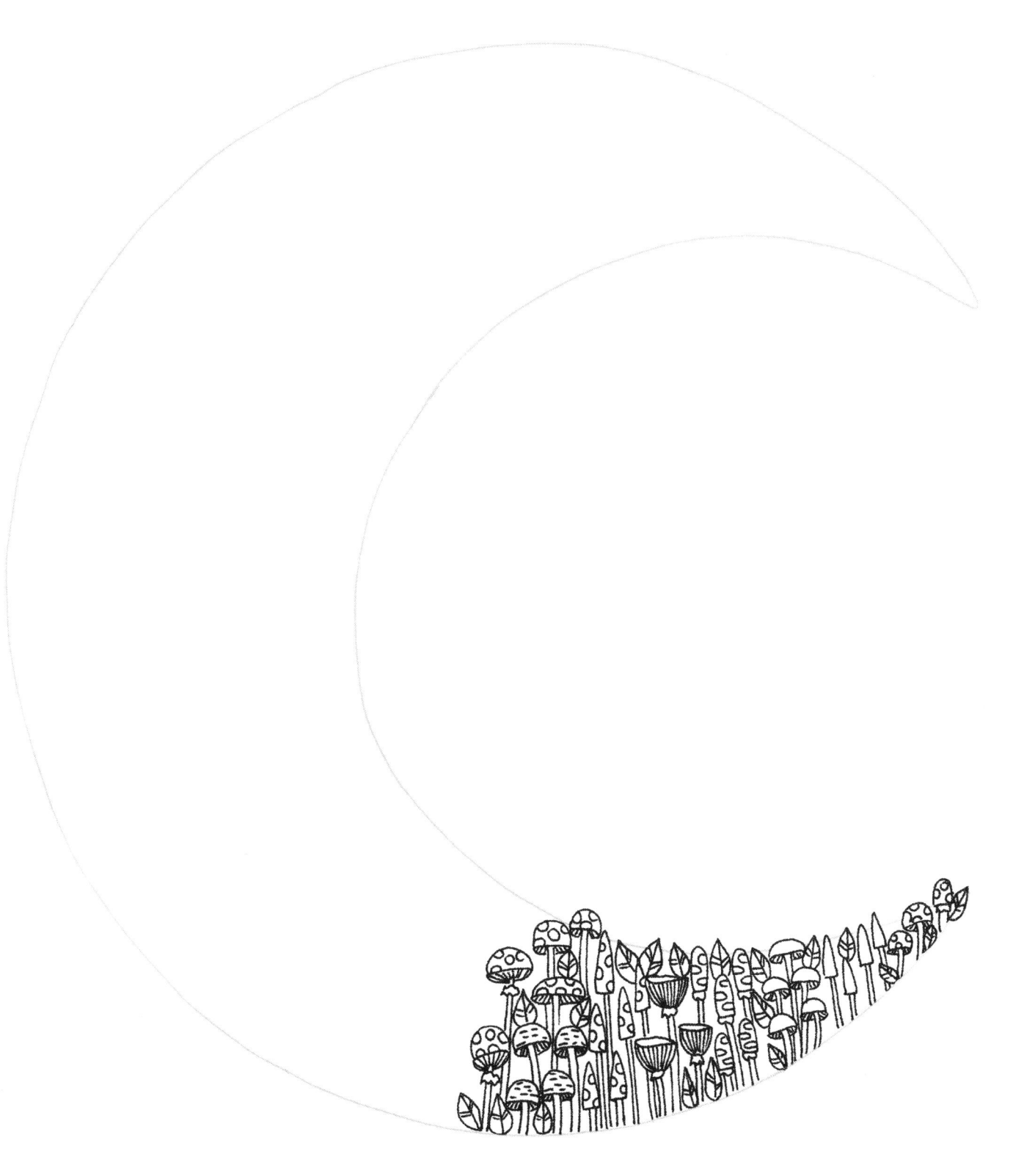

Frog pond

This drawing looks really complicated, as there are so many different shapes, but just take your time. As you work your way up the paper, think constantly about where you're going to position the next element. Are you going to partially hide a frog behind two leaves or show all of it? Will the flowers overlap the leaves or stand out from them? Remember to leave spaces in between, otherwise everything will look too cluttered and confusing and the individual elements won't stand out enough.

MATERIALS USED

- Fabriano 200gsm heavyweight paper
- Graphite pencil
- Faber-Castell Ecco Pigment 0.1mm black fineliner pen
- Faber-Castell Pitt Artist Pens (colors 109, 112, 113, 129, 131, 167, 170, 171, 172, 174, 239, 264)

Master the basics

For the frogs, begin with the eyes (1). Then draw the rounded body shape, with the eyes protruding above it, and block in the pupils of the eyes (2). Add the front legs (make the fingers "wiggly") (3), the back legs (4), and finally the mouth to give your frogs some expression and character (5).

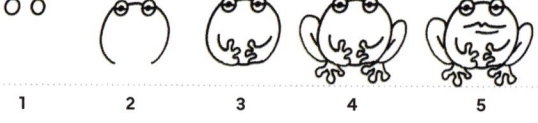

1   2   3   4   5

The flowers are drawn in a similar way to many others in this book, but pay attention to the shapes of the petals.

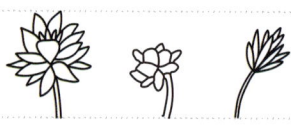

Draw the lily pads at different angles—some curving to one side, some bent over.

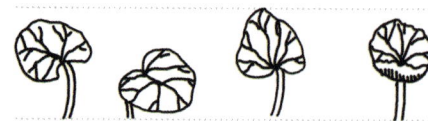

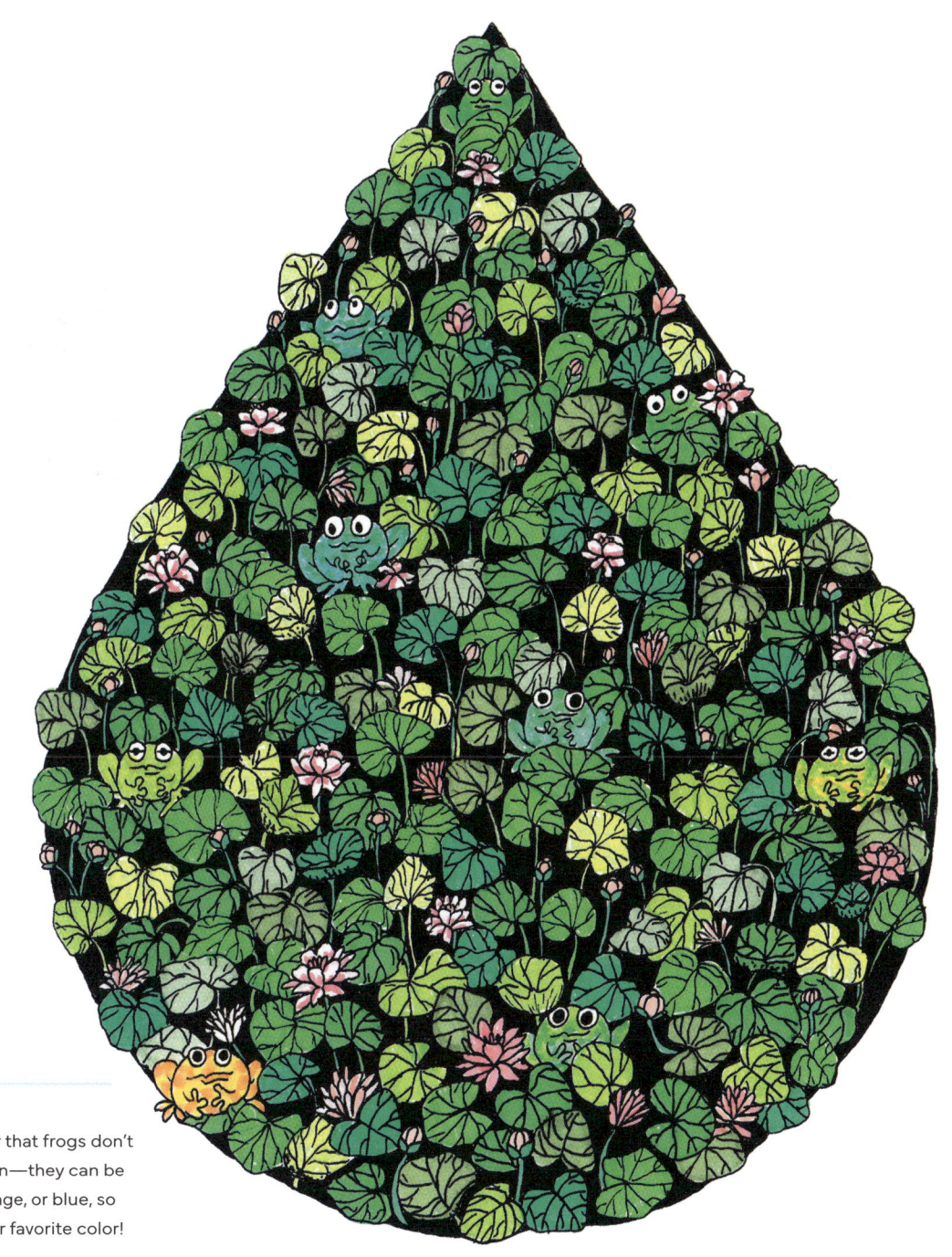

TIP Remember that frogs don't have to be green—they can be yellow, red, orange, or blue, so just choose your favorite color!

Drawing practice

How to draw and color key shapes

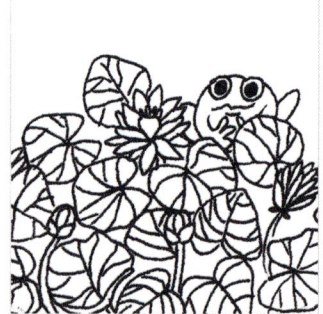

1 Start with drawing the pond outline, then begin filling it by drawing a couple of lily pads leaning in toward each other. Add a frog above; you can draw just the body, if you like, so that it looks as if the frog is peering out from behind the foliage.

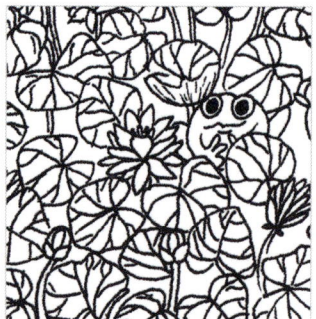

2 Work methodically and slowly as you fill the rest of the space, taking care to leave small gaps between the various shapes. When you've filled the pond, stand back and assess it all. Have you remembered to include some water lily flowers, and veins on all the leaves?

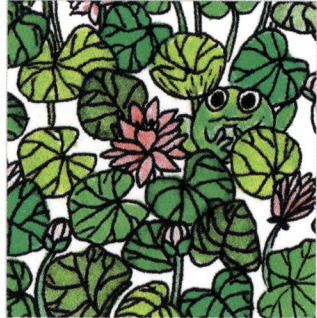

3 Start coloring the frogs. I used mostly blues and greens, but I added one orange frog for a really vibrant splash of color. Then color in the lily pads and flowers. I used a range of yellows and greens for the lily pads and pinks for the flowers, so that they'd contrast well with each other.

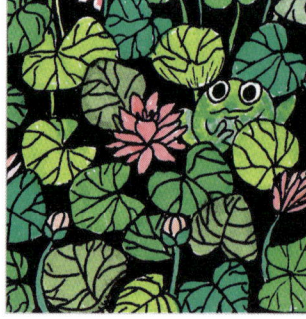

4 Leave the background until last. You can either fill it with black, as I did, or with blue to imitate the water.

Practice here

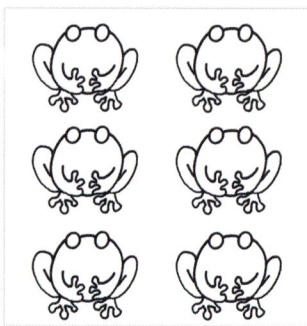

Add different eyes and mouths to these frogs.

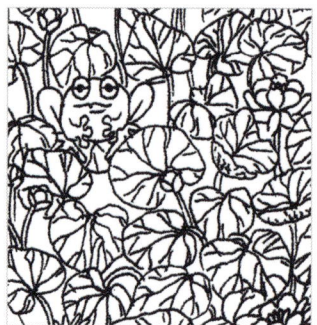

Color the elements in this box, remembering to use two colors or tones for the frogs.

Fill this outline.

TIP If you find that frogs are too complicated, just draw the eyes and part of the body peeping out from behind the lily pads—or draw dragonflies instead, which are an easier shape.

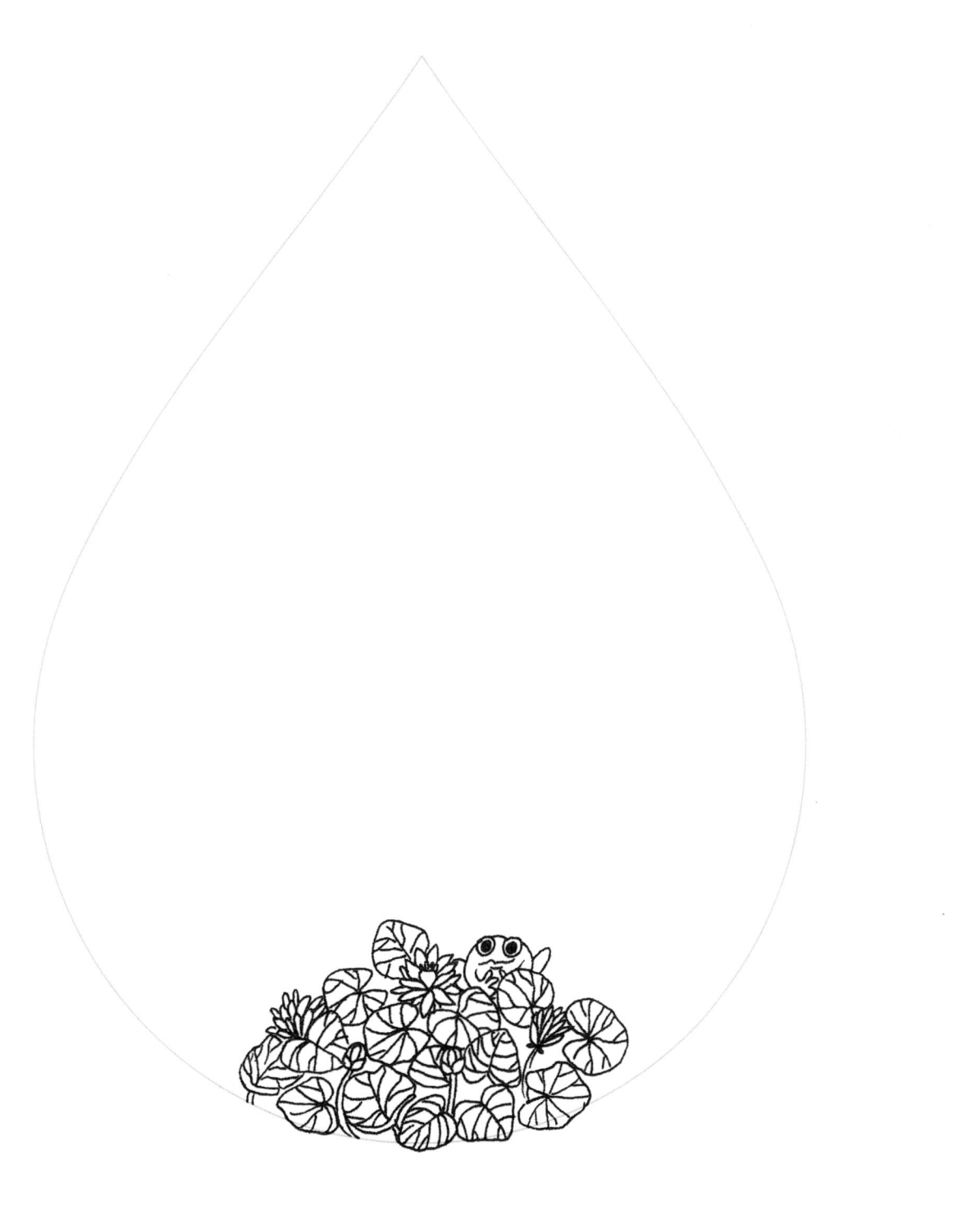

Letter A

Drawing letters can be great fun—you can create a wonderful, magical world enclosed in a letter! Use it to decorate your room or your child's room, or give it to someone as the perfect gift. You can use any colors or patterns to create your work of art, so look through the patterns you've learned in this book and choose the one that best suits the recipient's tastes or interests, or devise a pattern of your own.

MATERIALS USED

· Fabriano 200gsm heavyweight paper
· Graphite pencil
· Staedtler 0.1mm black fineliner pen
· Faber-Castell Pitt Artist Pens (colors 107, 109, 112, 113, 120, 121, 125, 133, 134, 136, 143, 148, 156, 162, 167, 170, 174, 192, 219, 239, 272, 273)

Master the basics

This design draws together various elements that you have learned in previous projects to create a magical forest scene. However, these four shapes may feel new to you, so use the blank lines here to practice drawing these leaves and flowers—or create your own unique shapes in this space instead!

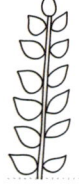

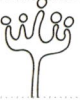

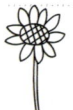

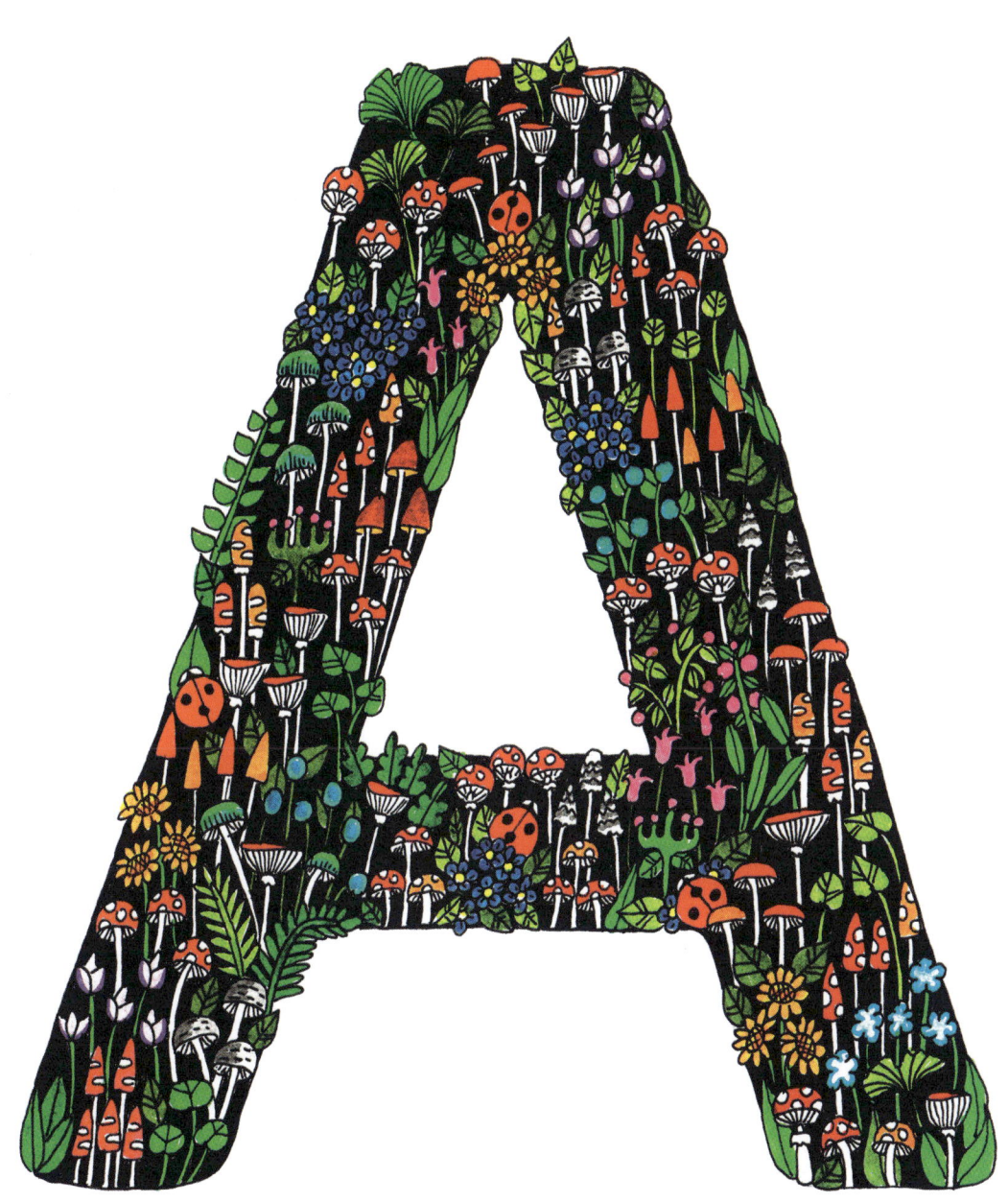

Drawing practice

How to draw and color key shapes

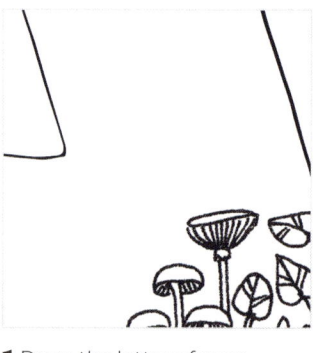  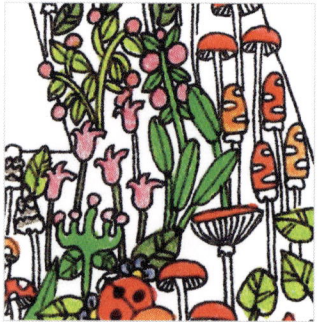 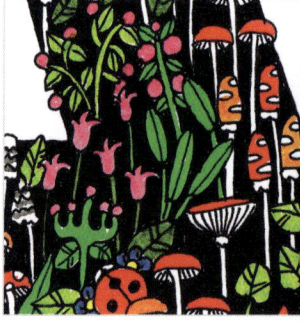

1 Draw the letter of your choice using a graphite pencil. Start filling the letter with patterns, working from the bottom up. I went for a woodland theme of fungi and flowers that I've used in other designs, but feel free to choose your own.

2 Include a few ladybugs, too. Remember that you can play with the scale in your patterns—I made my ladybugs bigger than the mushrooms and flowers, just for fun.

3 Go over the pencil lines in black fineliner then begin coloring, using your warm pink and red colors first if you're following my pattern. Then move on to the yellows and greens for the remaining flowers and foliage.

4 Finally, put in the background. I used black to make the other colors stand out more, but choose one that contrasts the most with the colors you used.

Practice here

 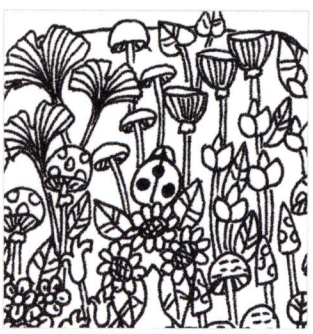 

Design your own flowers, mushrooms, or leaves.

Experiment with a color palette.

Fill this outline with your chosen designs.

TIP Fonts come in many different styles, from simple outlines like the ones you find on children's building blocks to more cursive, rounded forms that are meant to resemble handwriting. If you can't decide on the style of your letter, search online for one that you like—but for something like this, it's generally best to opt for a sans serif font, as they have bold, instantly recognizable outlines, giving you plenty of space to fill with your chosen pattern.

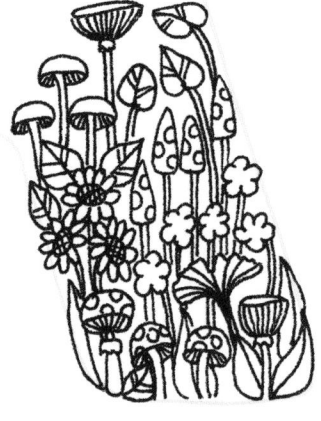

Snails on a leaf

Did you ever collect snails after the rain? As a child, I could walk around the garden for hours looking for snails for my snail farm. (Don't worry, they all survived and were released after a few weeks!)

I wanted to do something special and combine them with a leaf from my favorite tree: *Ginkgo biloba*. Did you know that this is a tree that has been in existence for over 200 million years? It is also called a living fossil.

This drawing also includes tiny flowers filling the gaps between the snails. Think carefully about which colors to use so that the flowers don't become too dominant, as the snails are the stars of the show here. Make the snail shells really vibrant and the flowers more muted in tone.

MATERIALS USED

- Fabriano 200gsm heavyweight paper
- Graphite pencil
- Faber-Castell Eco Pigment 0.1mm black fineliner pen
- Faber-Castell Pitt Artist Pens (colors 107, 120, 127, 136, 143, 167, 170, 171, 186, 264, 268, 272, 273)

Master the basics

Drawing a snail isn't too difficult. Start by drawing a spiral for the shell (1), then add the body, varying the size and shape a bit (2). Draw the antennae, with the eyes at the tip (3). Add another snail facing in the opposite direction and fill the gap in between with tiny five-petaled flowers, which you've already seen in other drawings in this book.

Choose a vibrant color palette for the shells to make each snail stand out from its neighbors—I went with the full rainbow here!

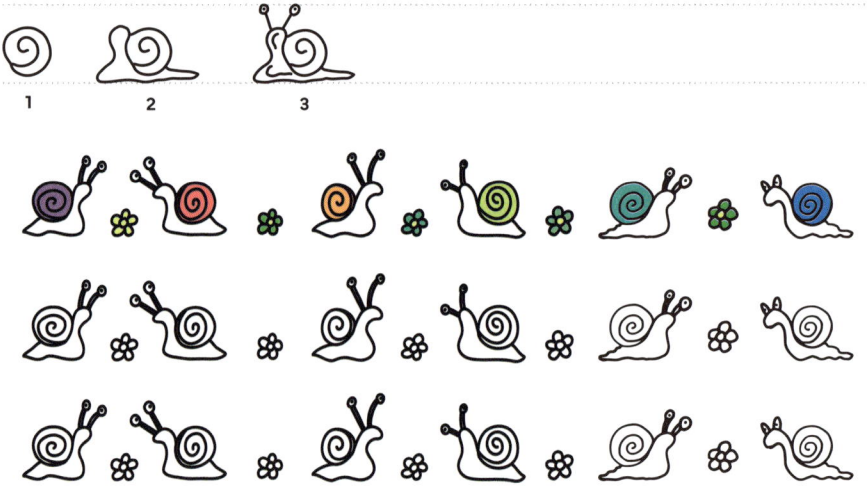

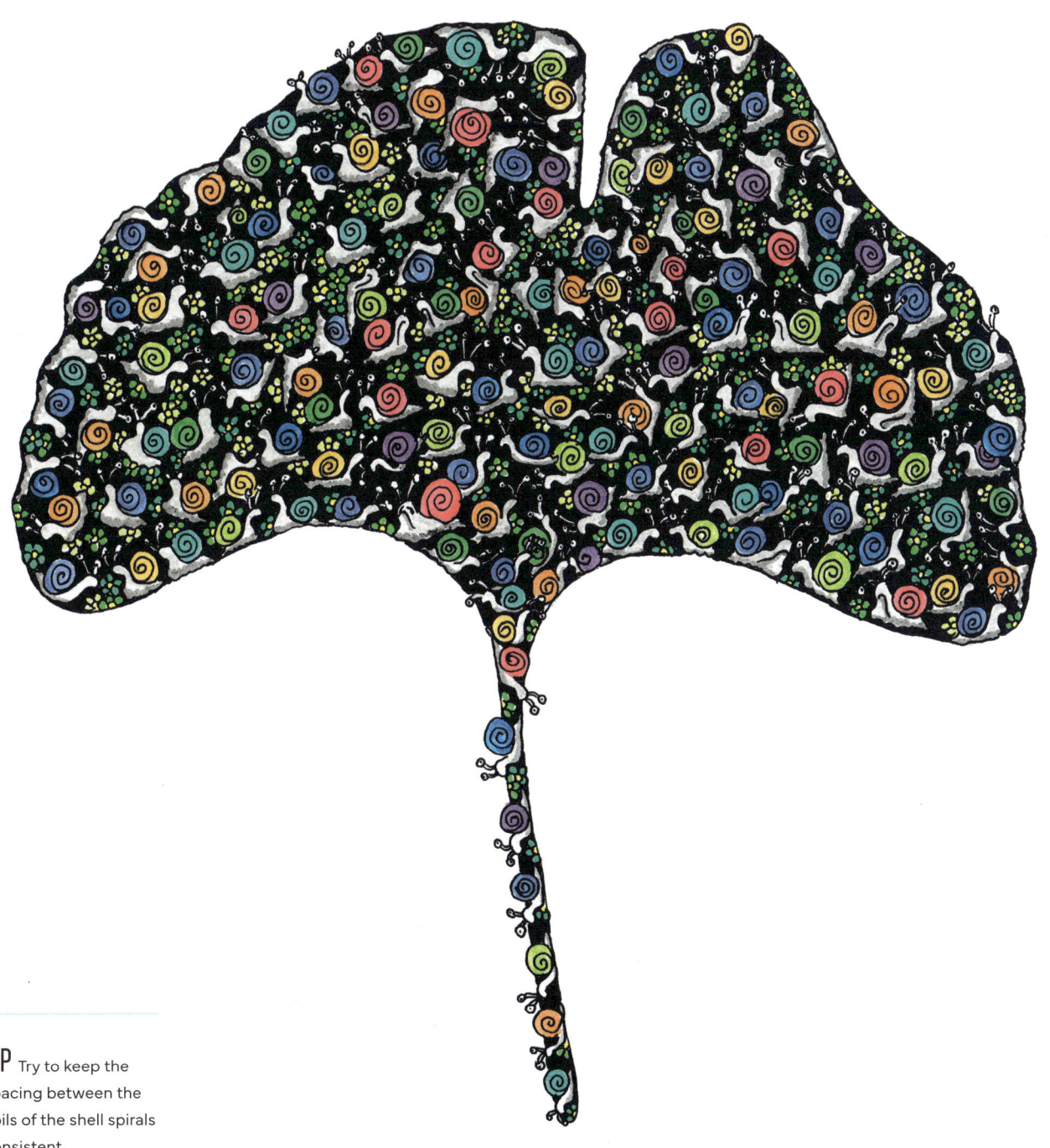

TIP Try to keep the spacing between the coils of the shell spirals consistent.

Drawing practice

How to draw and color key shapes

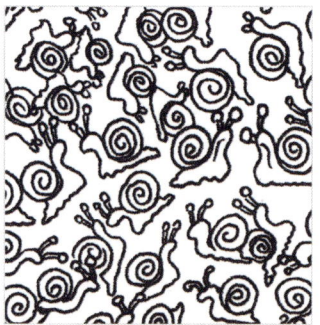

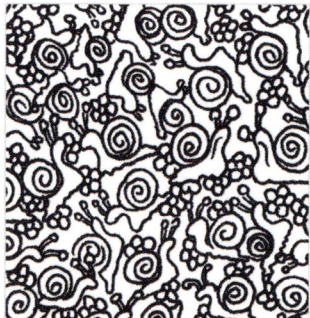

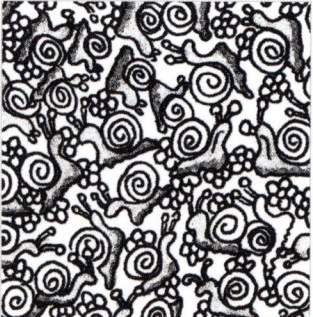

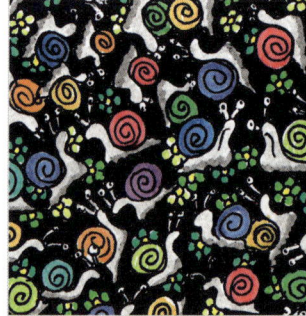

1 Start with drawing the leaf outline. Begin filling the leaf with snails, starting from the base and working your way up. Vary the direction in which the snails face. Continue until you've filled the whole leaf, varying the shapes and size of the snails.

2 Between the snails draw some small five- or six-petaled flowers. Go over your pencil lines with black fineliner.

3 Carefully shade the underside of the snails' bodies, using a soft, light gray. Take care not to press too hard: you want this shading to be very subtle so that it will still stand out from the dark background color.

4 Color in the snails' shells and the flowers. You can let your imagination run wild here and make the snails really vibrant! As always, leave the background until the very end. You can fill it with black, like I did, or green for a more natural leaf look.

Practice here

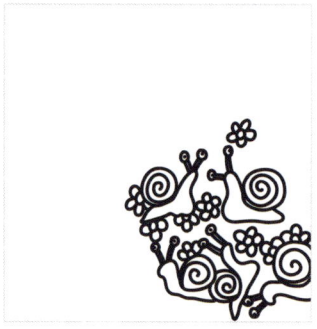

Continue filling this box with snails and flowers.

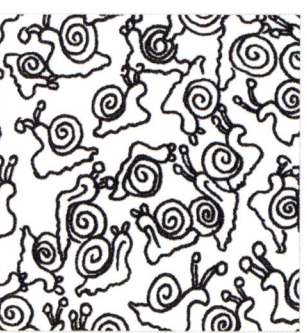

Add flowers—or even hearts— between these snails.

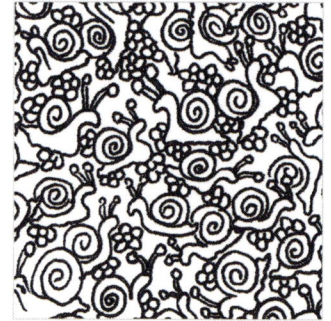

Color in these snails using your chosen color palette.

TIP Practice shading the snails' bodies on scrap paper before you color in the drawing. It's important not to press too hard, as you want a light tone here.

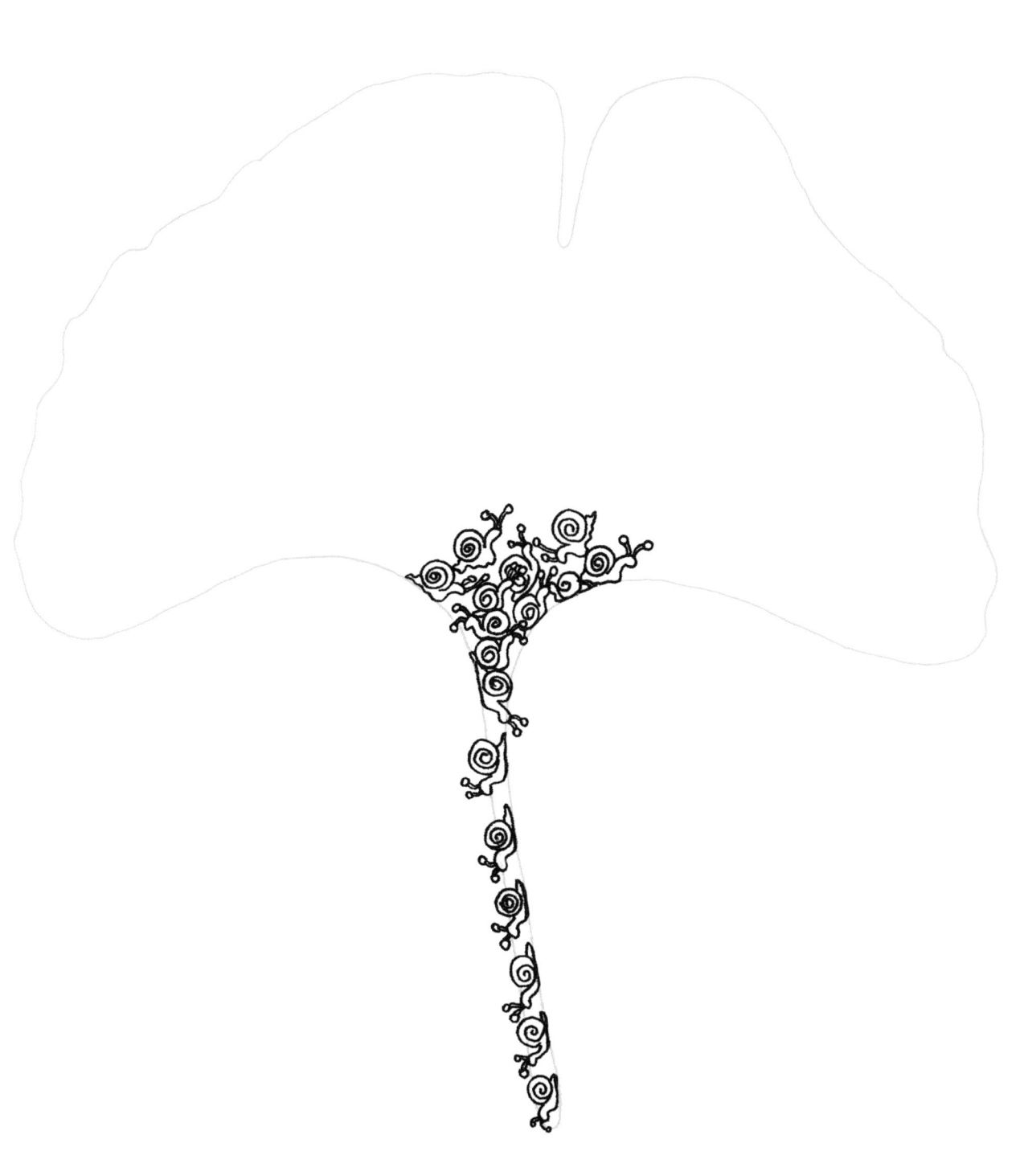

Cherry blossom moon

A pleasant spring evening was the inspiration for this drawing. The crescent moon and the smell of cherry blossoms in my parents' garden always put me in a good mood—and when they were no longer with me in this world, the drawing became a source of valuable memories.

Cherry blossom petals are very delicate, with subtle gradations of color. Watercolor paints or pencils are perfect for this, but colored pencils work brilliantly, too: allow your pencil to just skim the surface for the lightest areas around the centers of the petals and apply a little more pressure and/or build up several layers toward the outer edges, where you want a darker tone.

MATERIALS USED

- Fabriano 200gsm heavyweight paper
- Graphite pencil
- Rotring 0.2mm technical pen
- Ecoline watercolor inks (numbers 350, 381, 390) or Faber-Castell Pitt Artist Pens (colors 112, 114, 125, 129, 131, 132)
- Uni Posca PC-1M white marker pen

Master the basics

Cherry blossom flowers: Draw the center of the flower first (1), then draw irregularly shaped petals around it (2-3). Go back to the center and draw the tiny circles of the stamens (4), then add attaching lines down the middle of each petal (5). Start drawing the next flower between the petals of the first one and repeat the same actions (6-7).

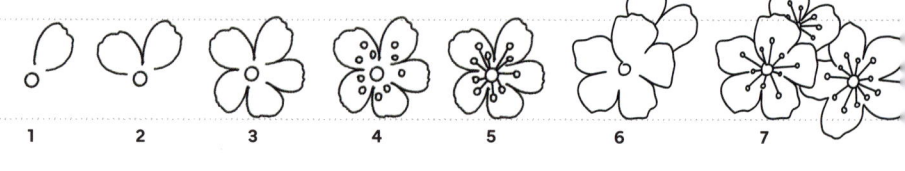

Cherry blossom buds: Start by drawing a short stem and two leaves (1), and then add a semi-oval on top (2). Finally, add two curved lines from the top of the semi-oval down to the leaves, to create the individual bud petals (3).

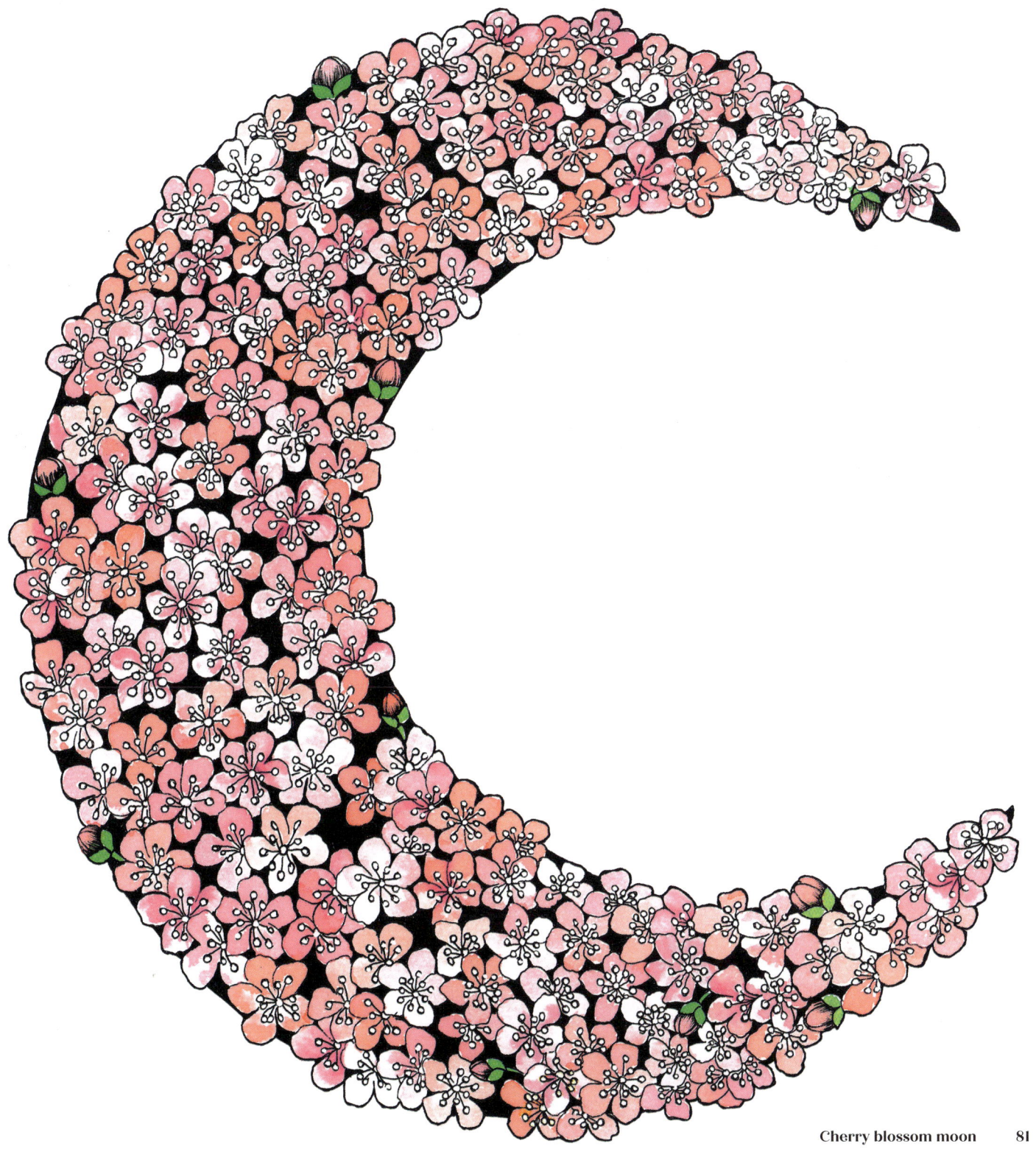

Cherry blossom moon   81

Drawing practice

How to draw and color key shapes

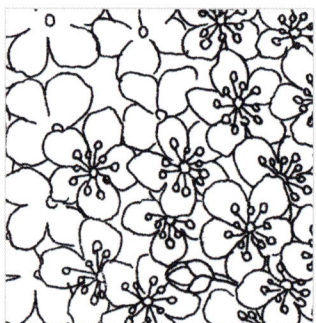

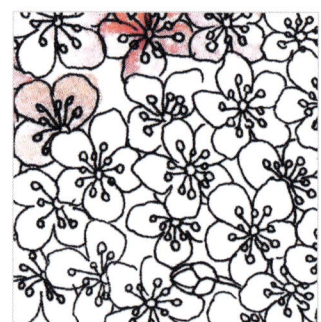

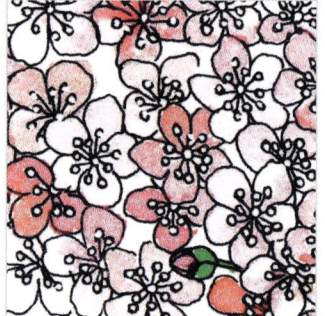

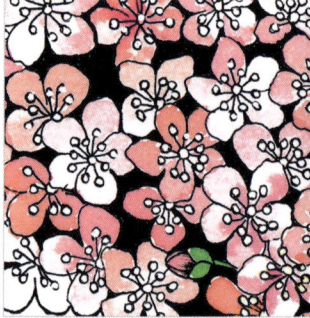

1 After drawing the crescent moon, start filling it with cherry blossoms and a few small flower buds, using a graphite pencil. Start at the bottom and work your way up. Be sure to leave small gaps between individual flowers to make the background more visible.

2 You can use color pens or watercolors to color the flowers, but whatever you choose, try to get some gradation of color into the petals so that they're darker toward the outer edges and paler toward the centers. Remember to leave the little circles at the tips of the stamens white.

3 When you've completed all the flowers, color the leaves green. Experiment to get the tone of green that works best—if it's too dark, it'll pop out too much and distract from the subtle pinks of the petals. If you've accidentally colored the tiny circles on the stamens, now's the time to correct this using a white marker pen.

4 Leave the background to the very end. The choice of background color is entirely up to you. I always prefer a black background, but a green background would look equally good with pink flowers.

Practice here

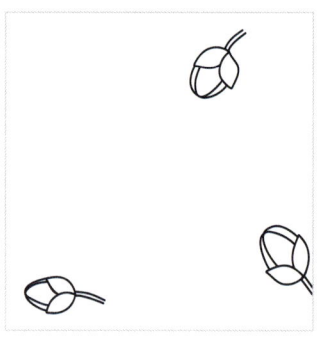

Add cherry blossoms around these buds.

Fill this outline with flowers.

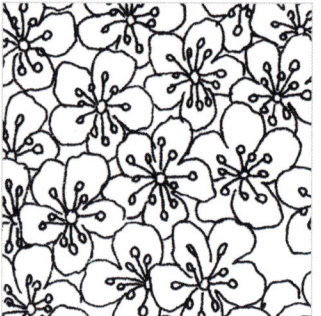

Color these flowers, perhaps trying a different background color.

TIP If you want to use watercolor paints to color the blossoms, practice this on a separate sheet of watercolor paper to ensure the paint properly adheres to the page.

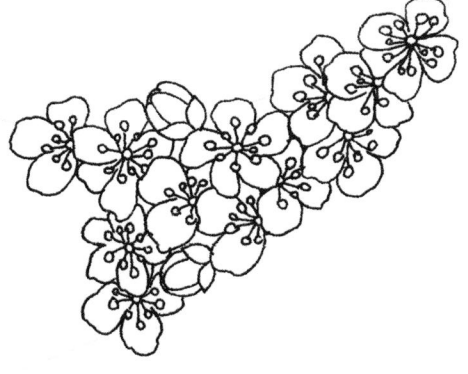

Letter H

For this project I chose a random letter and filled it with cats and dogs, to please the owners of both pets! Remember that this is not calligraphy but an exercise for your imagination. Start with a small letter and, as you practice, draw larger and larger ones. Then try drawing this same design in different letters. How does this change the way you approach the overall illustration? In time, perhaps you will even dare to transfer your drawings to canvas.

Drawing stimulates our imagination and creative thinking, helps calm our thoughts, and is the perfect hobby for rainy days. It has been a great pleasure to present to you my path to drawing. So don't wait: take a pencil and a piece of paper and show the world what you can do!

MATERIALS USED

- Fabriano 200gsm heavyweight paper
- Graphite pencil
- Staedtler 0.1mm black fineliner pen
- Faber-Castell Pitt Artists Pens (colors 104, 108, 109, 113, 121, 131, 132, 178, 180, 186, 188, 189, 192, 199, 232, 233, 272)

Master the basics

As with the rubber ducks (page 60), small changes to the eyes, mouth, or ears can create a whole range of different expressions. Here are a few ideas to get you started—you can replicate these dogs on the practice lines or on a separate sheet of paper, or experiment with different facial expressions or features.

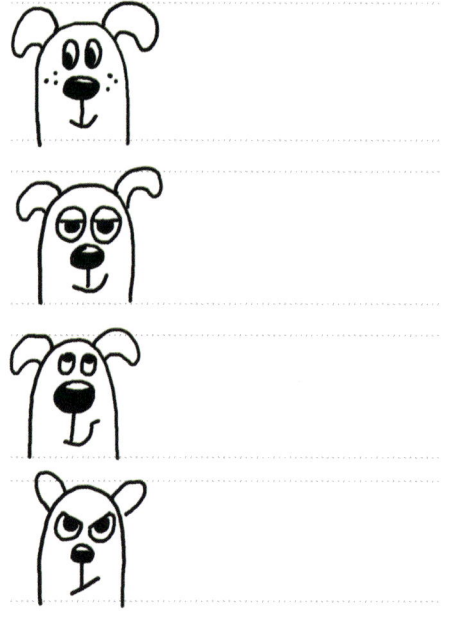
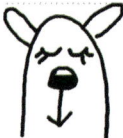
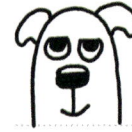
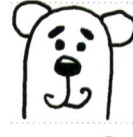
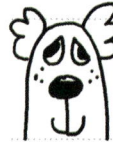

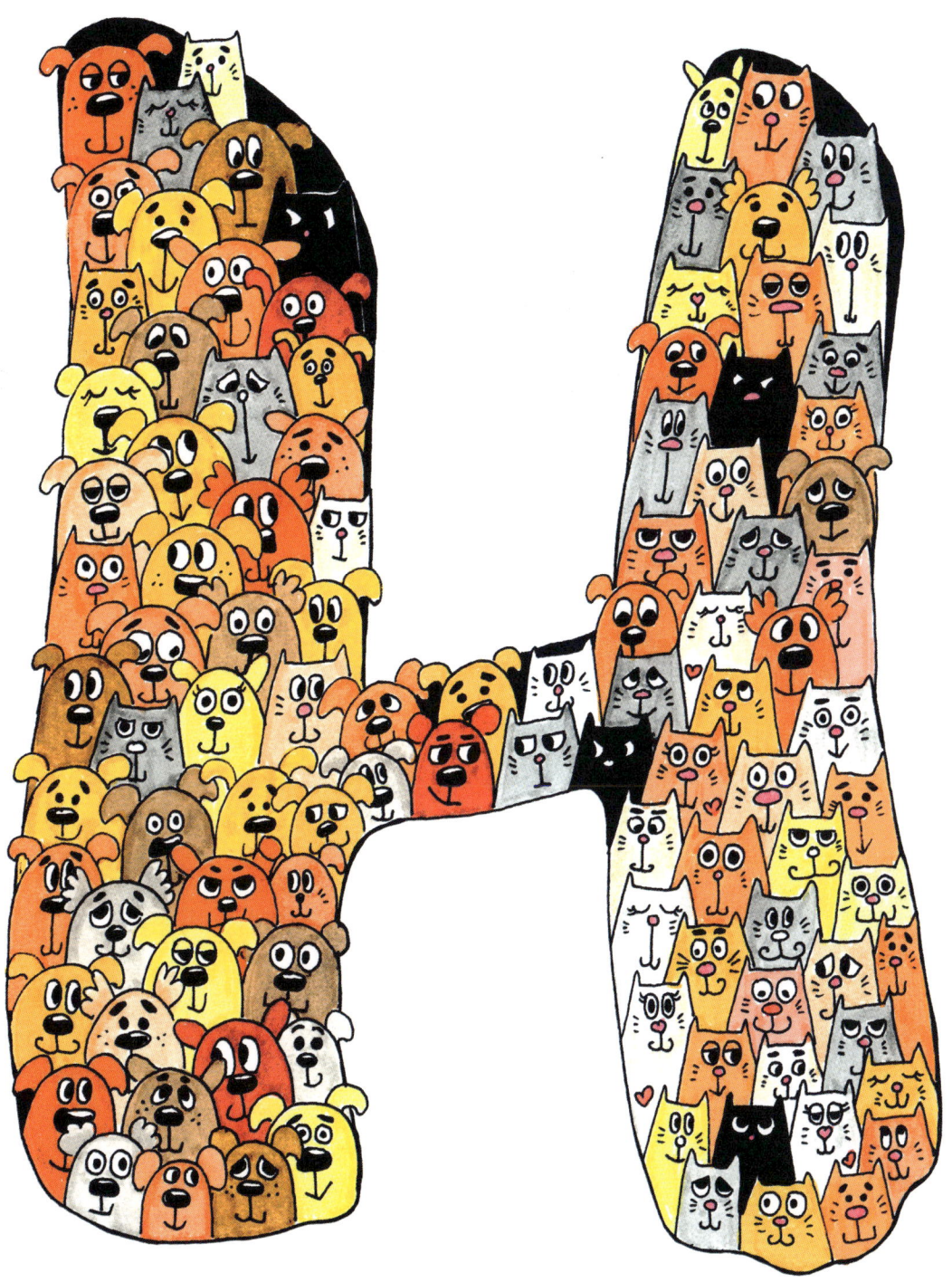

Drawing practice

How to draw and color key shapes

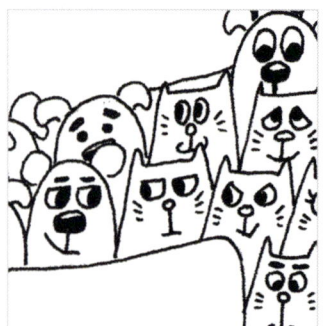 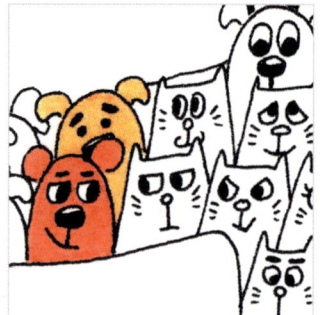 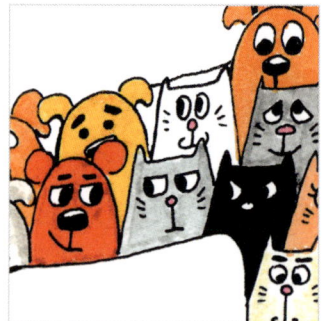 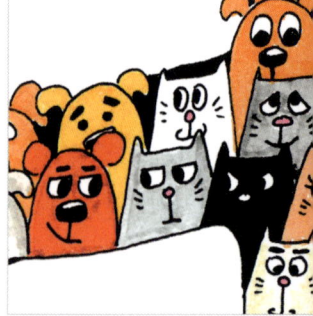

1 Draw the letter of your choice using a graphite pencil. Start filling the letter from the bottom up. I went for dogs on one side and cats on the other—the two don't always get along, so it seemed like a good idea to keep them separate at first!

2 Continue until you've filled the whole shape. I made the cats on the "bridge" between the two uprights of the letter H look slightly wary of their canine companions. Begin coloring, switching between dogs and cats so that you get a good overall balance of tones.

3 Leave a few of the animals white, if you like. Small pops of white or another very pale color can lighten the whole drawing and, in this case, make it easier to pick out individual animals' expressions.

4 Finally, put in the background. I used black to make the other colors stand out more, but that's entirely up to you. Congratulations—you have officially finished the last drawing of this book! I'm so proud of you! Now all that's left is to frame it nicely, decorate your home, and enjoy!

Practice here

 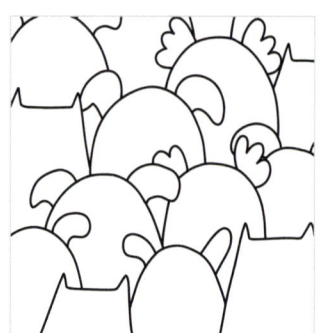 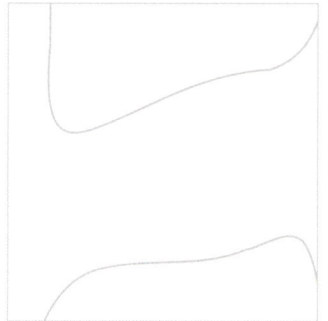

Draw your own dog and cat and give each a unique expression.

Fill these cat and dog outlines with faces.

Practice drawing cats and dogs in this shape.

TIP Remember to choose your palette before you start coloring—it will make it much easier and faster to finish the drawing.

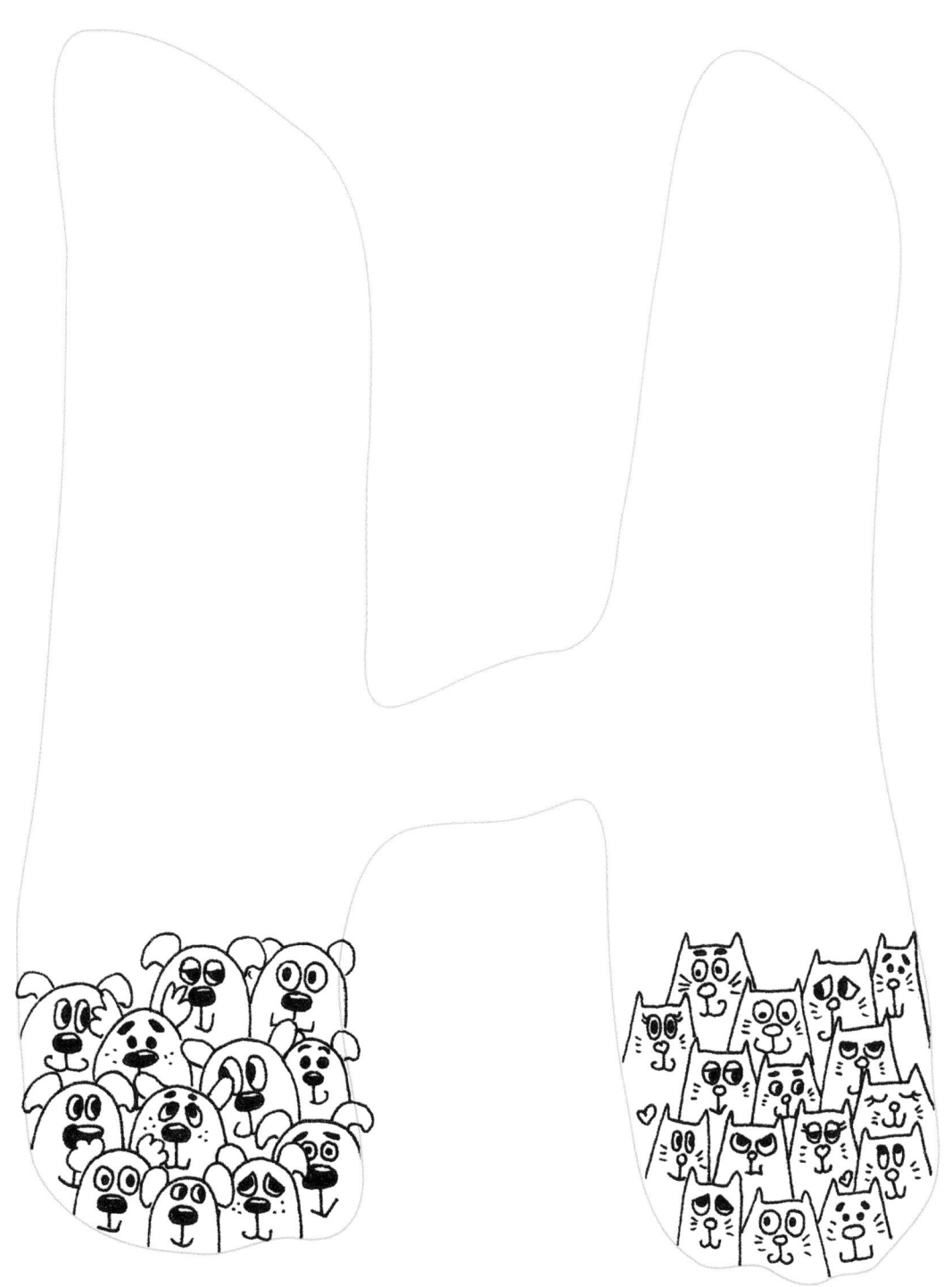

Drawings to color

In this section you'll find all 20 full-size drawings in black and white for you to color in as you choose. You could use them as practice pages and replicate my color palettes, or as blank canvases for your own experiments with color. Whatever option you choose, have fun with it—and don't forget to tear the pages out afterward and display your wonderful work!

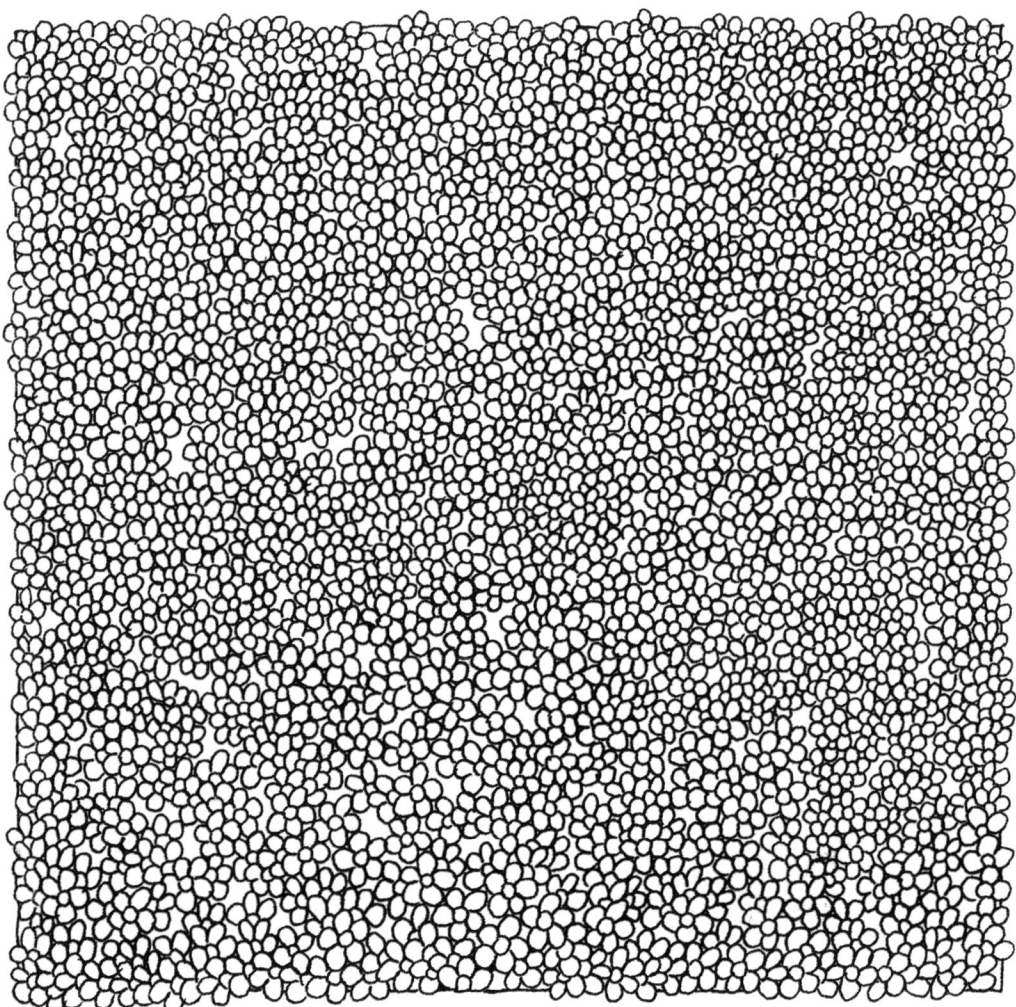

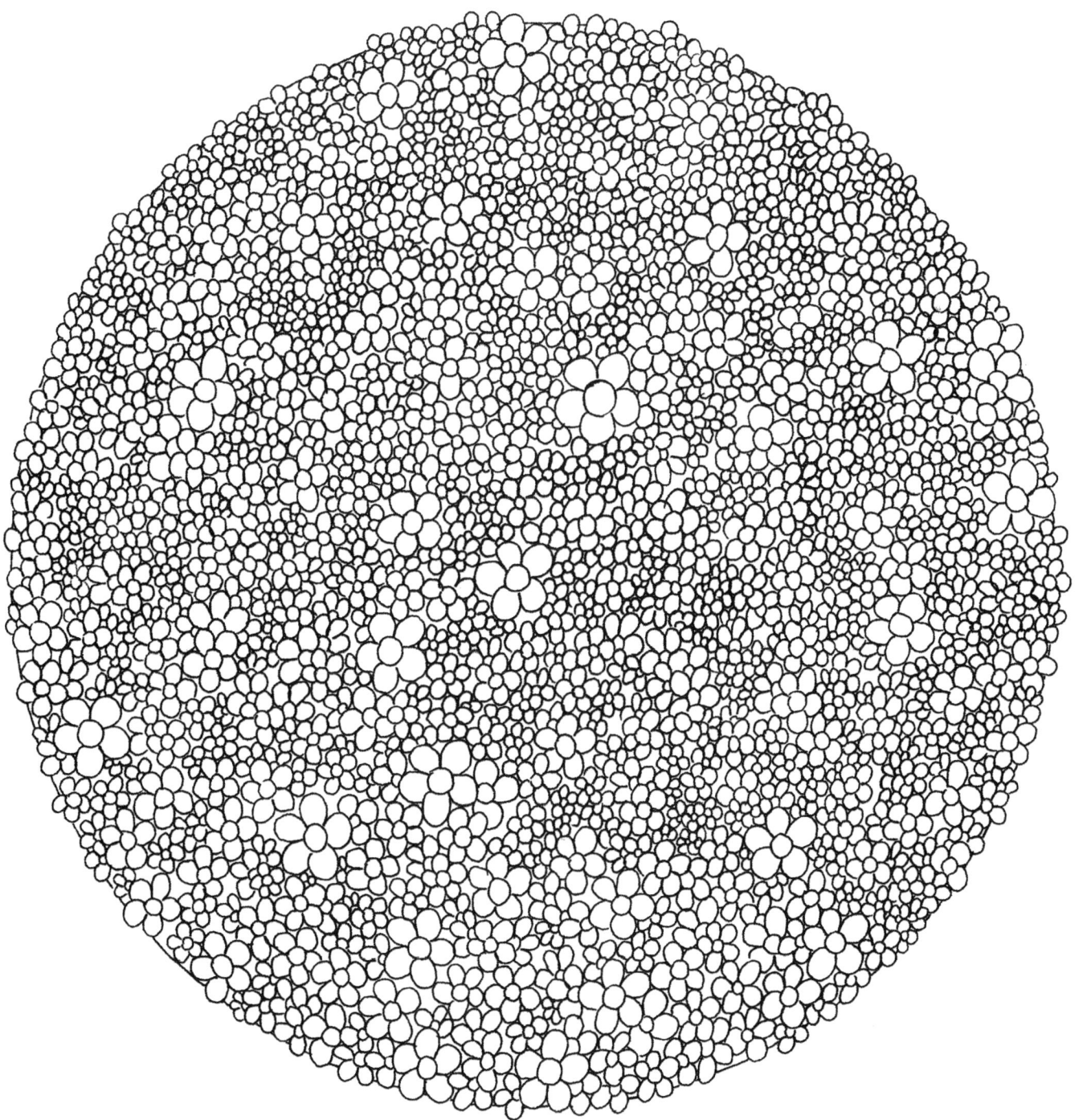

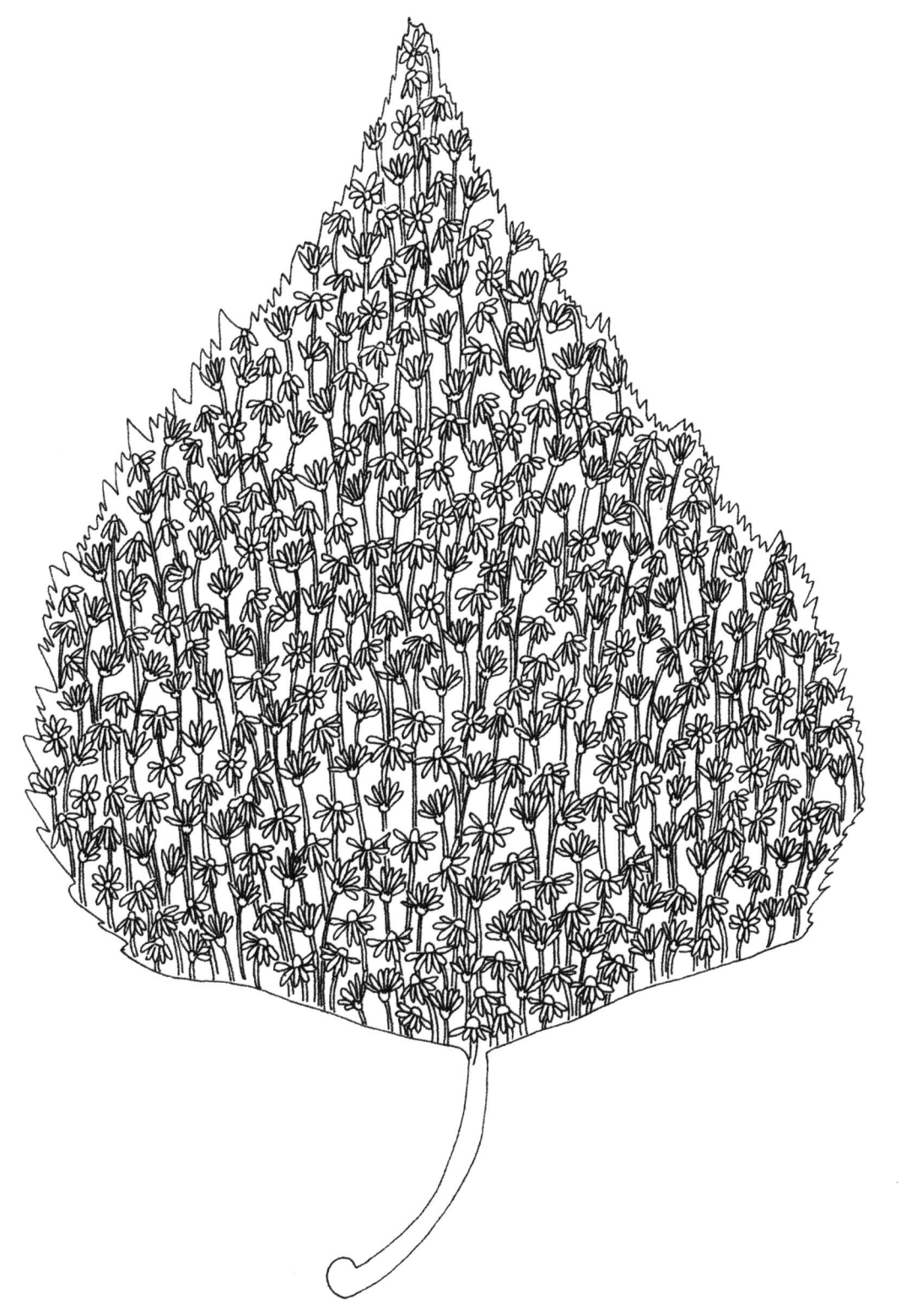

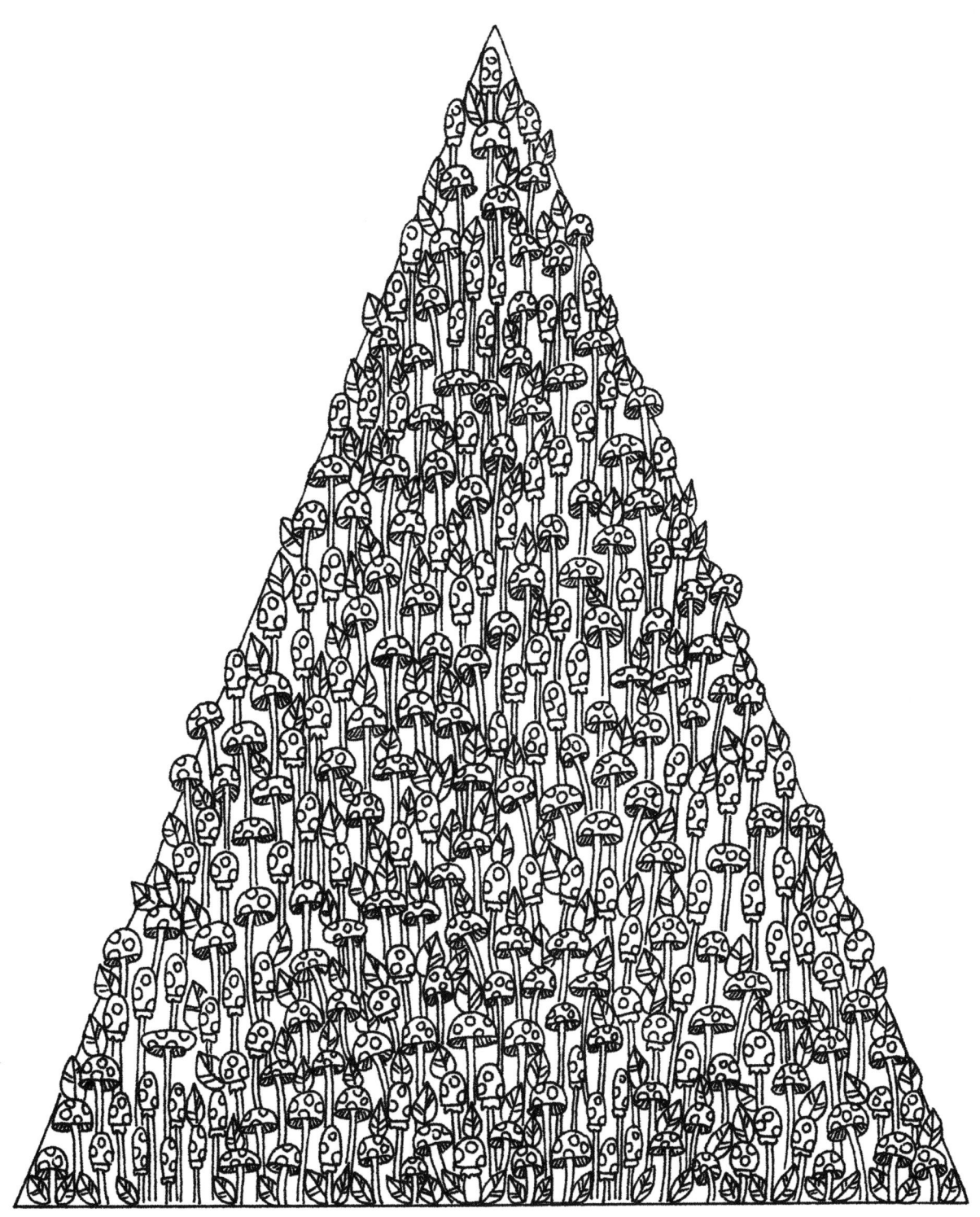

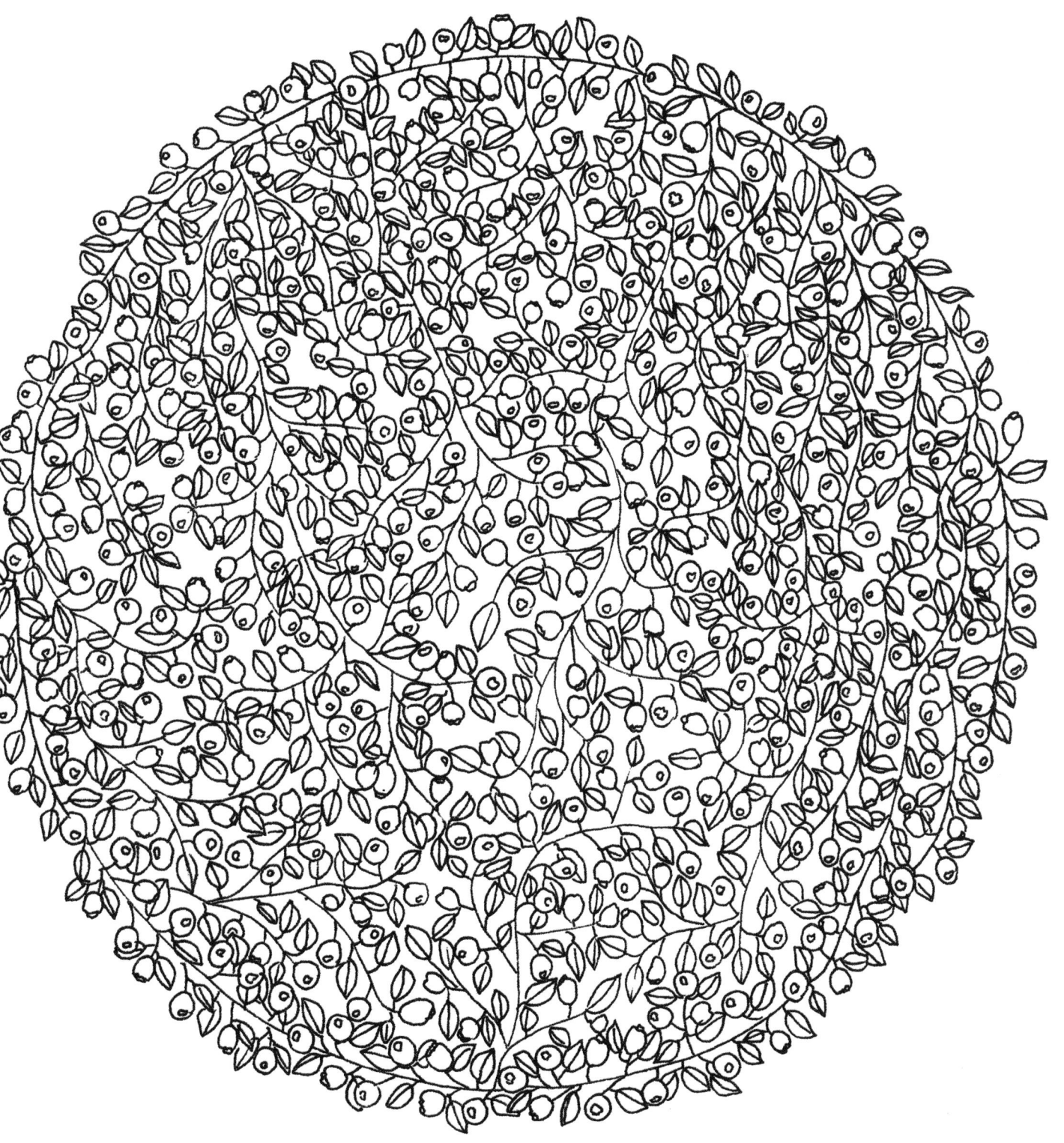

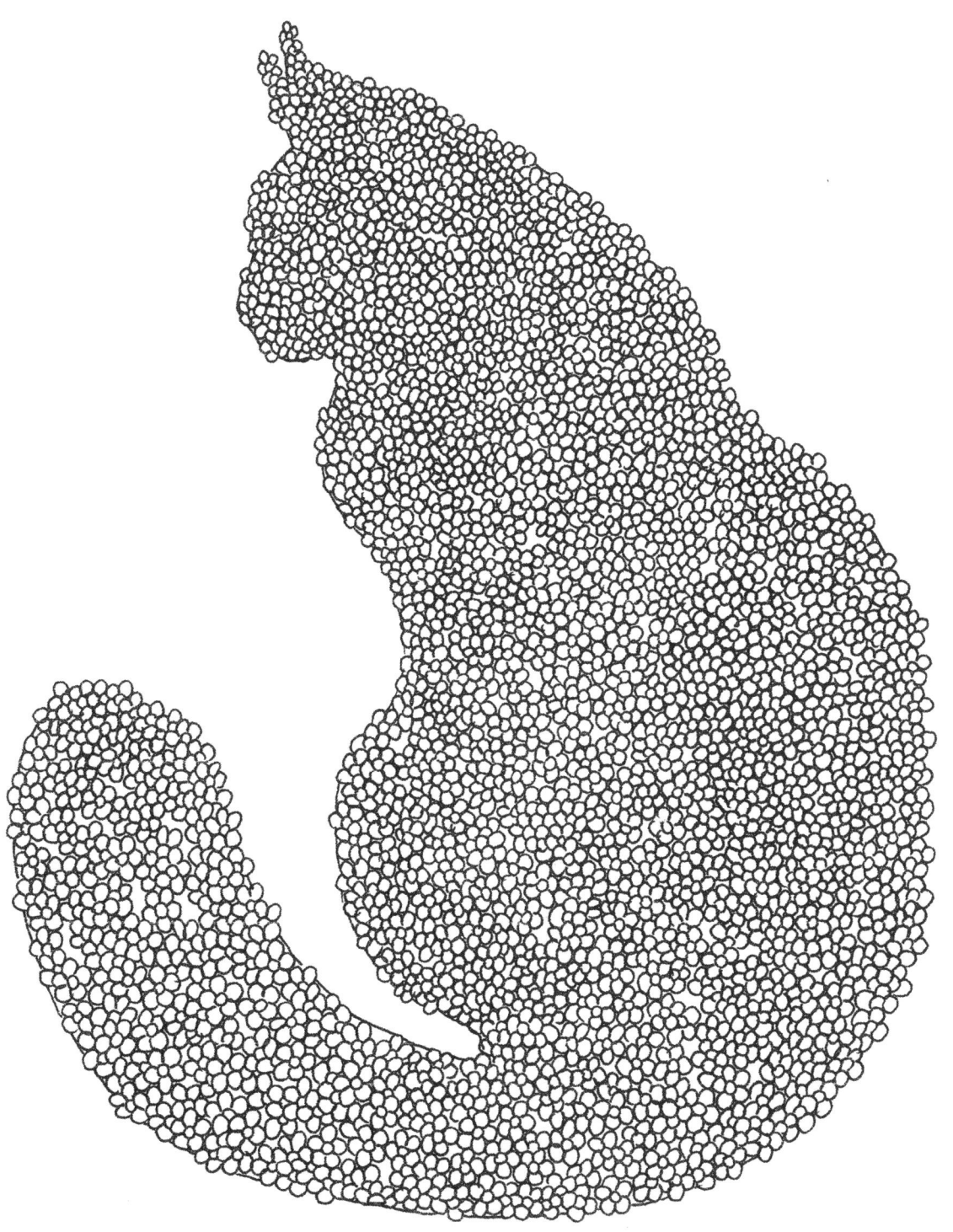

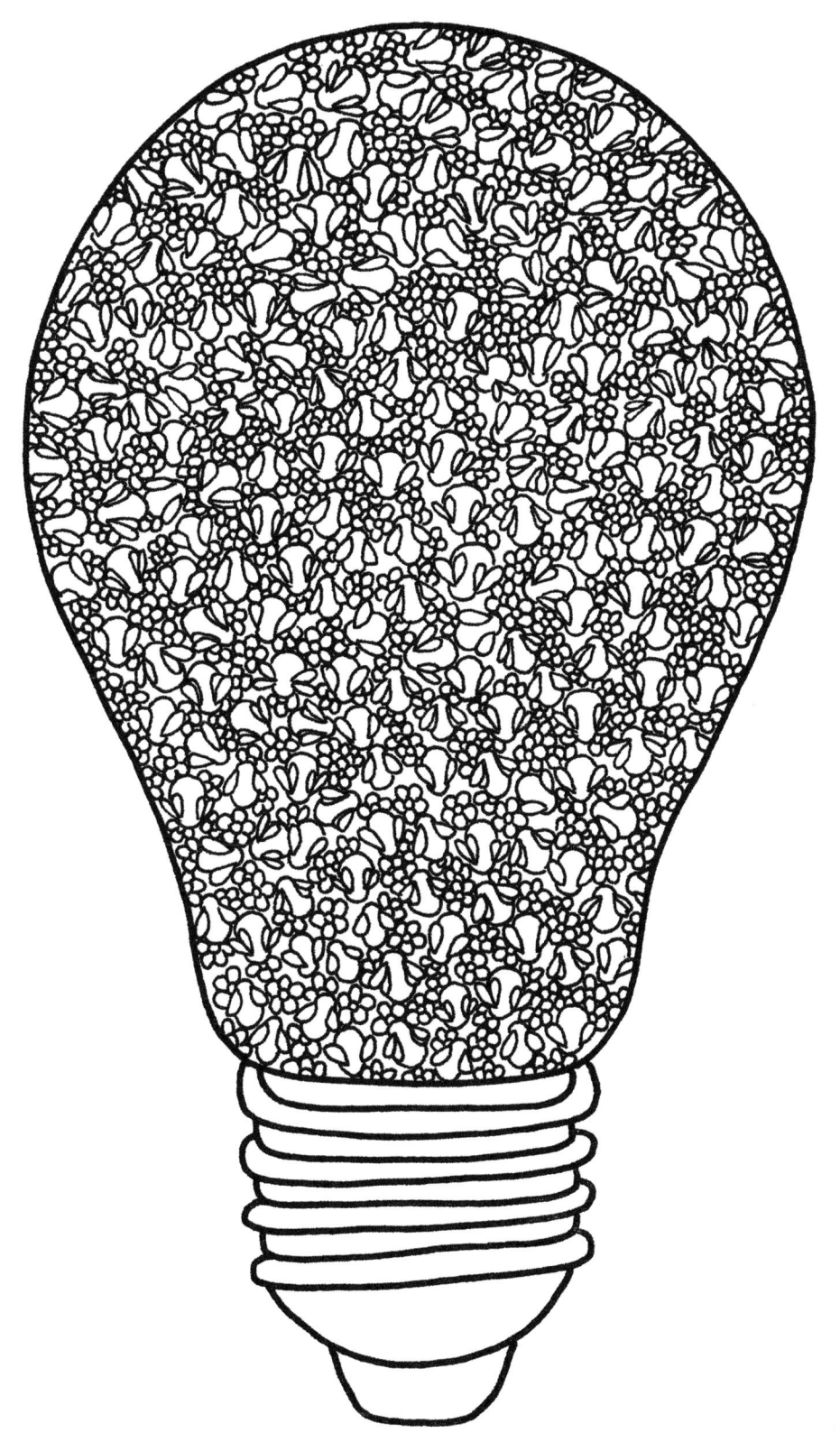

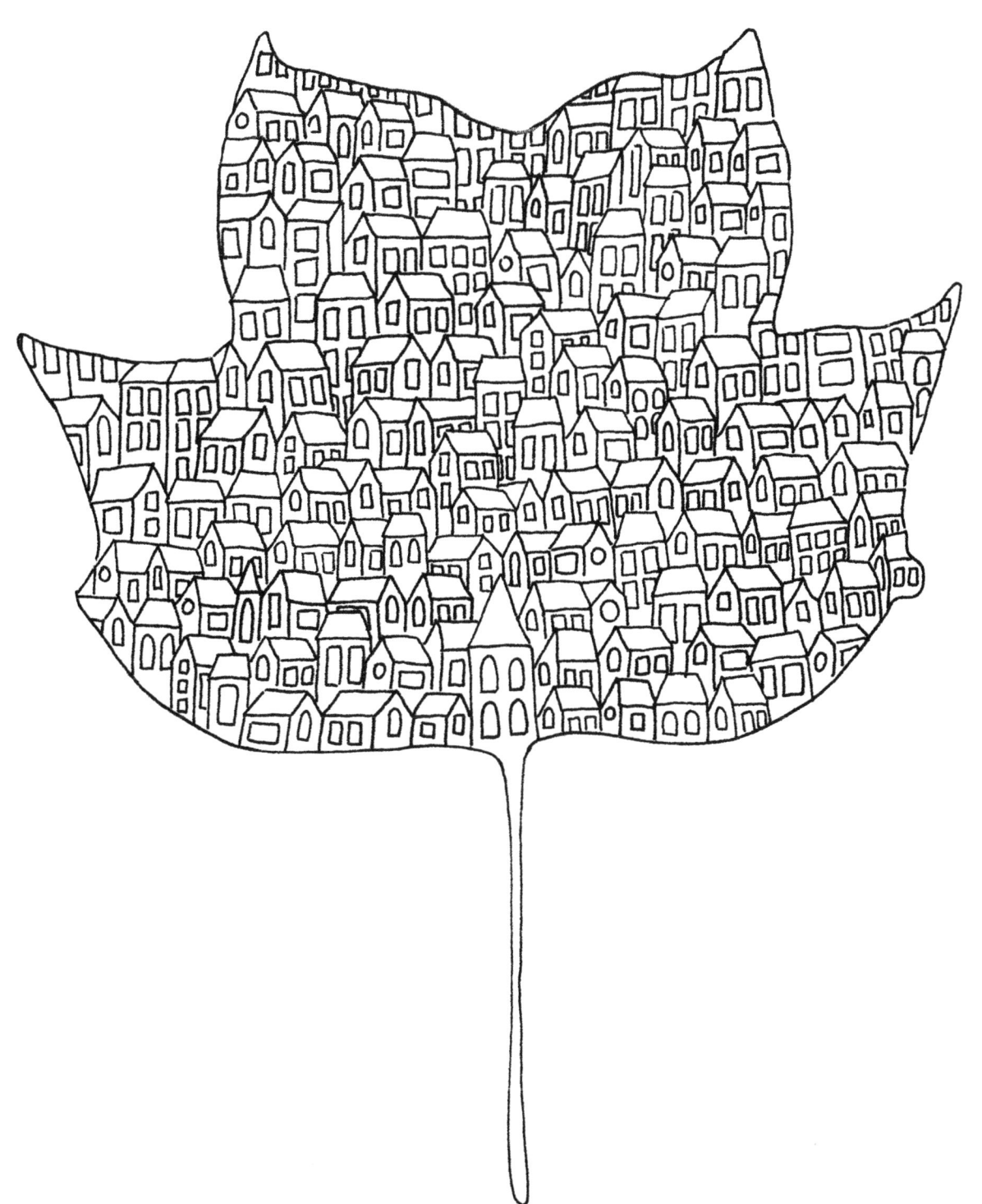

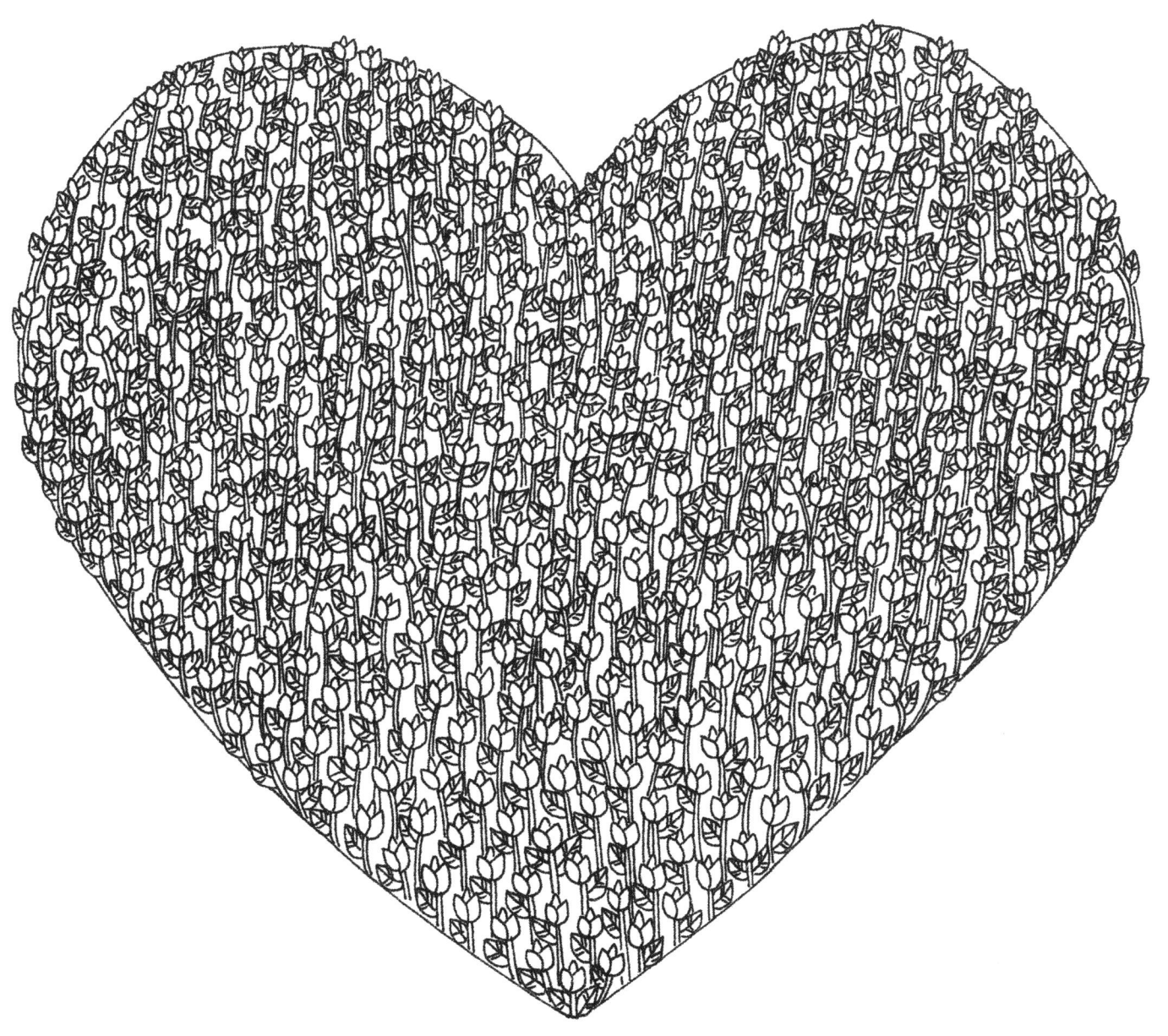

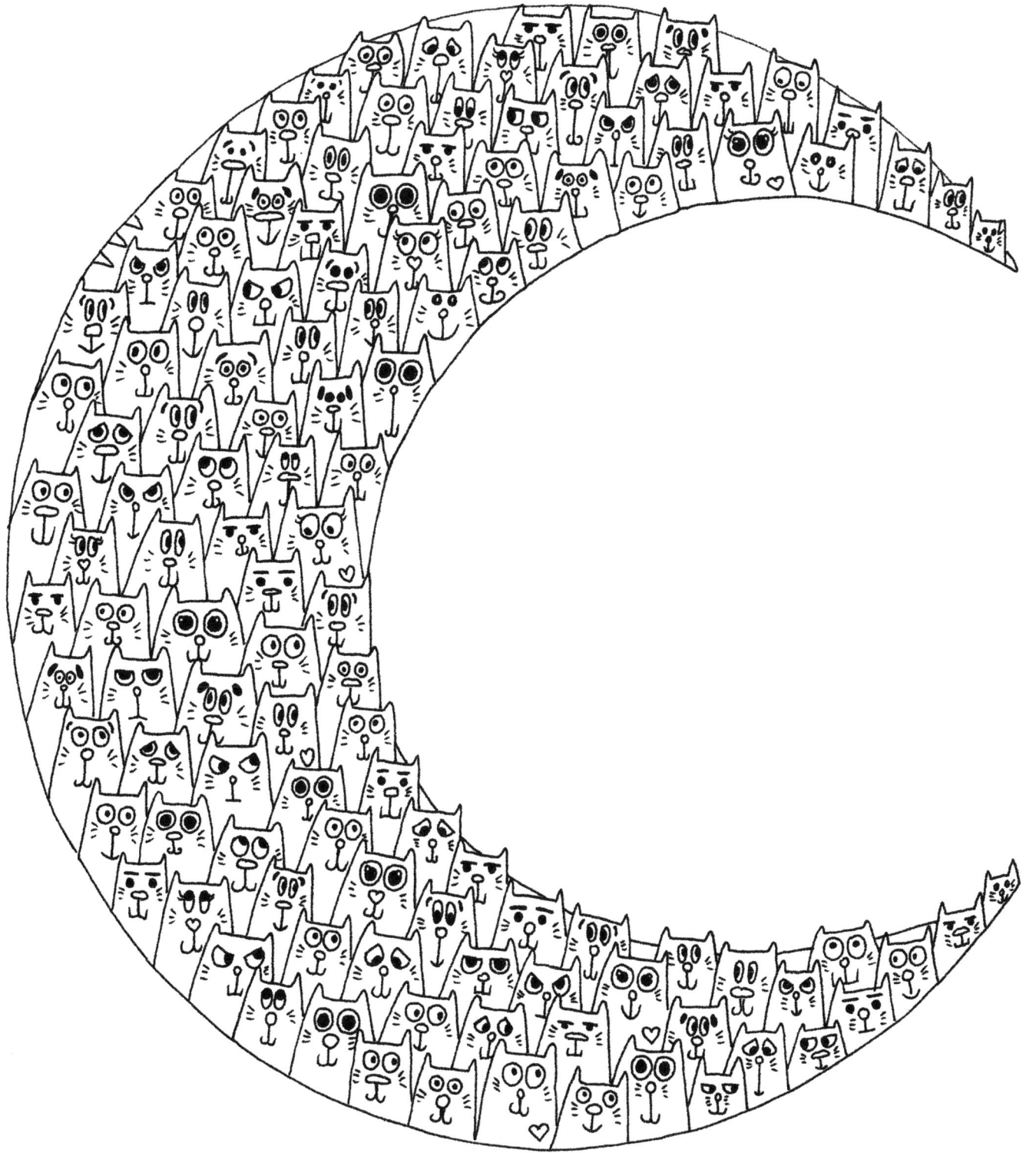

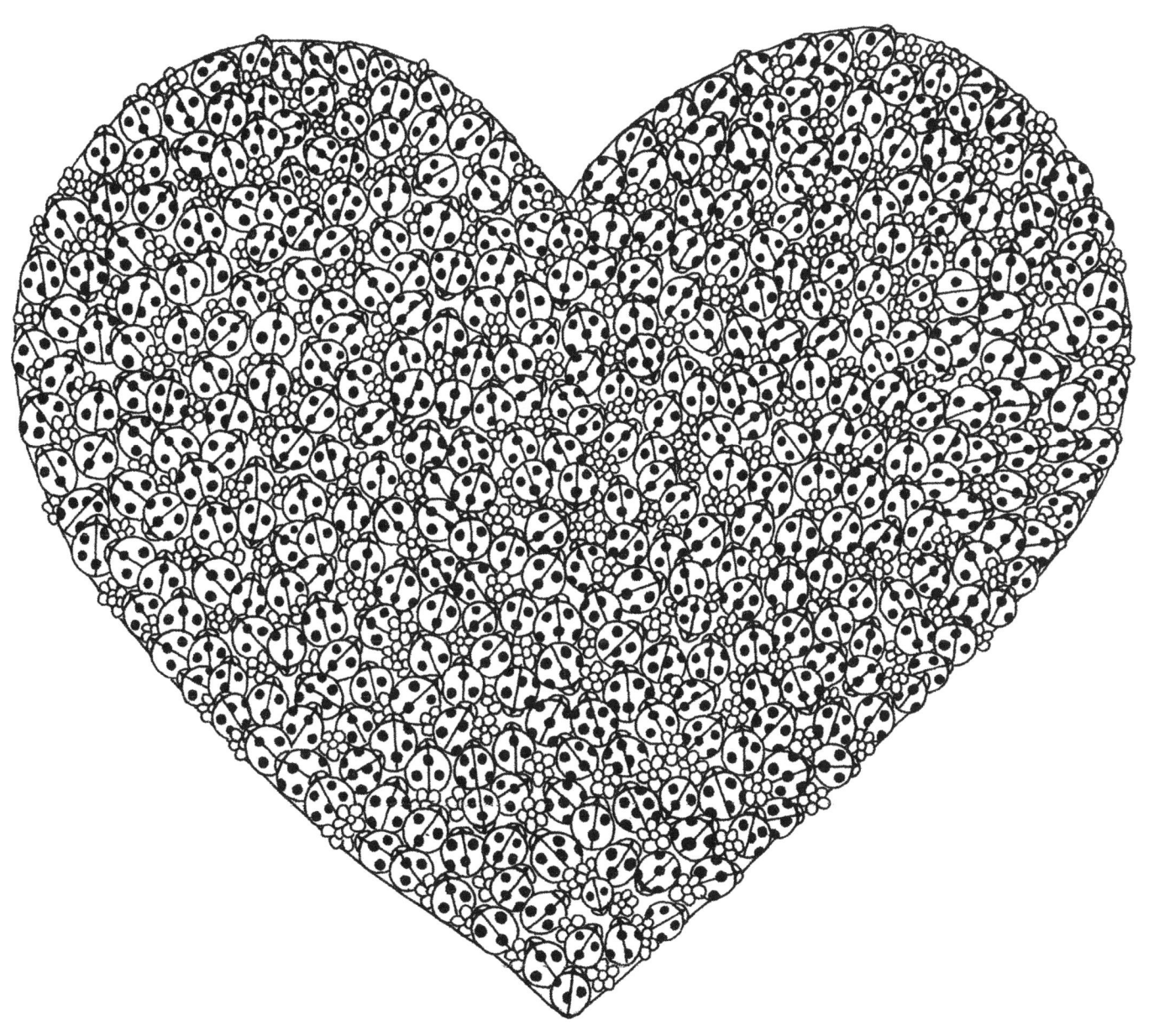

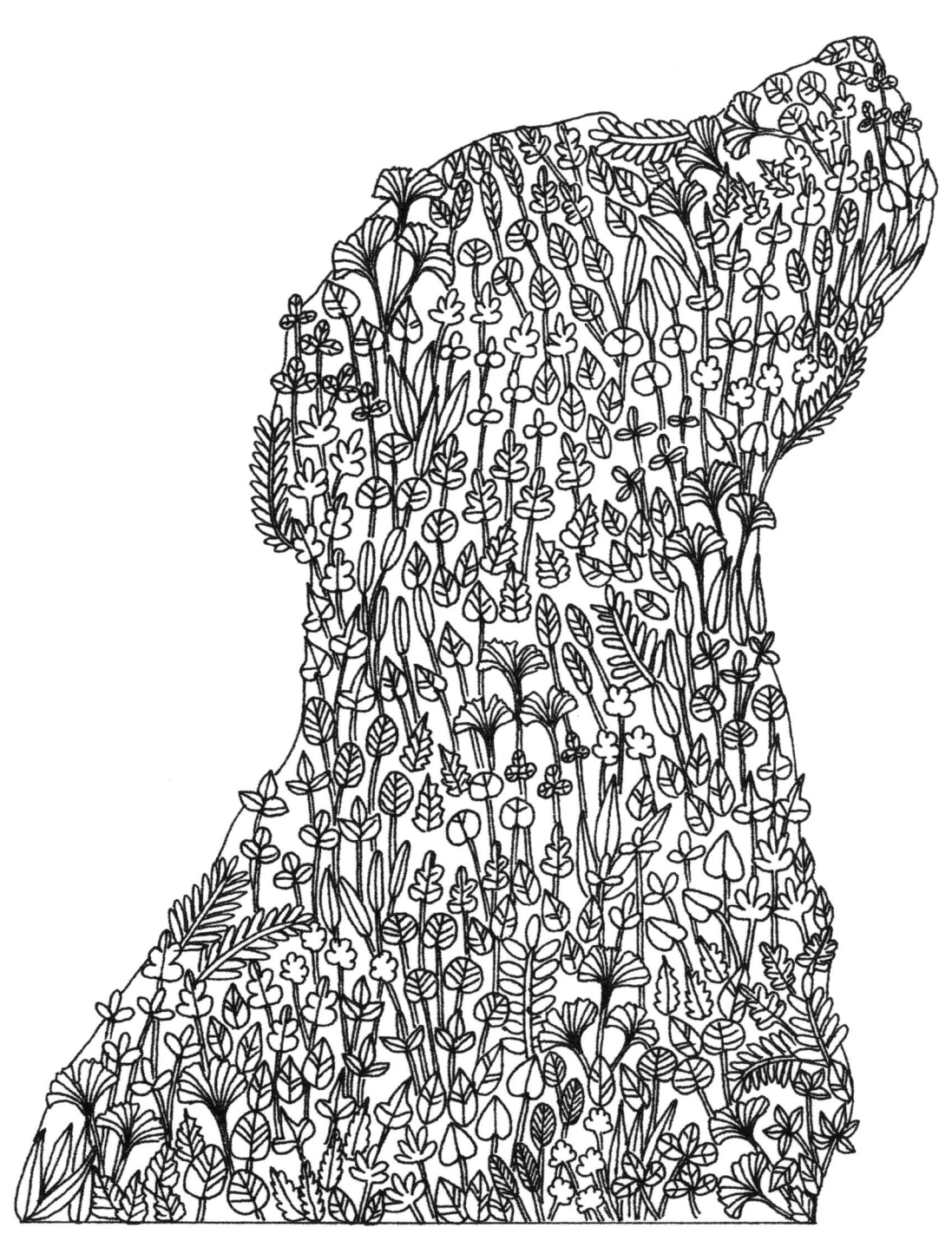

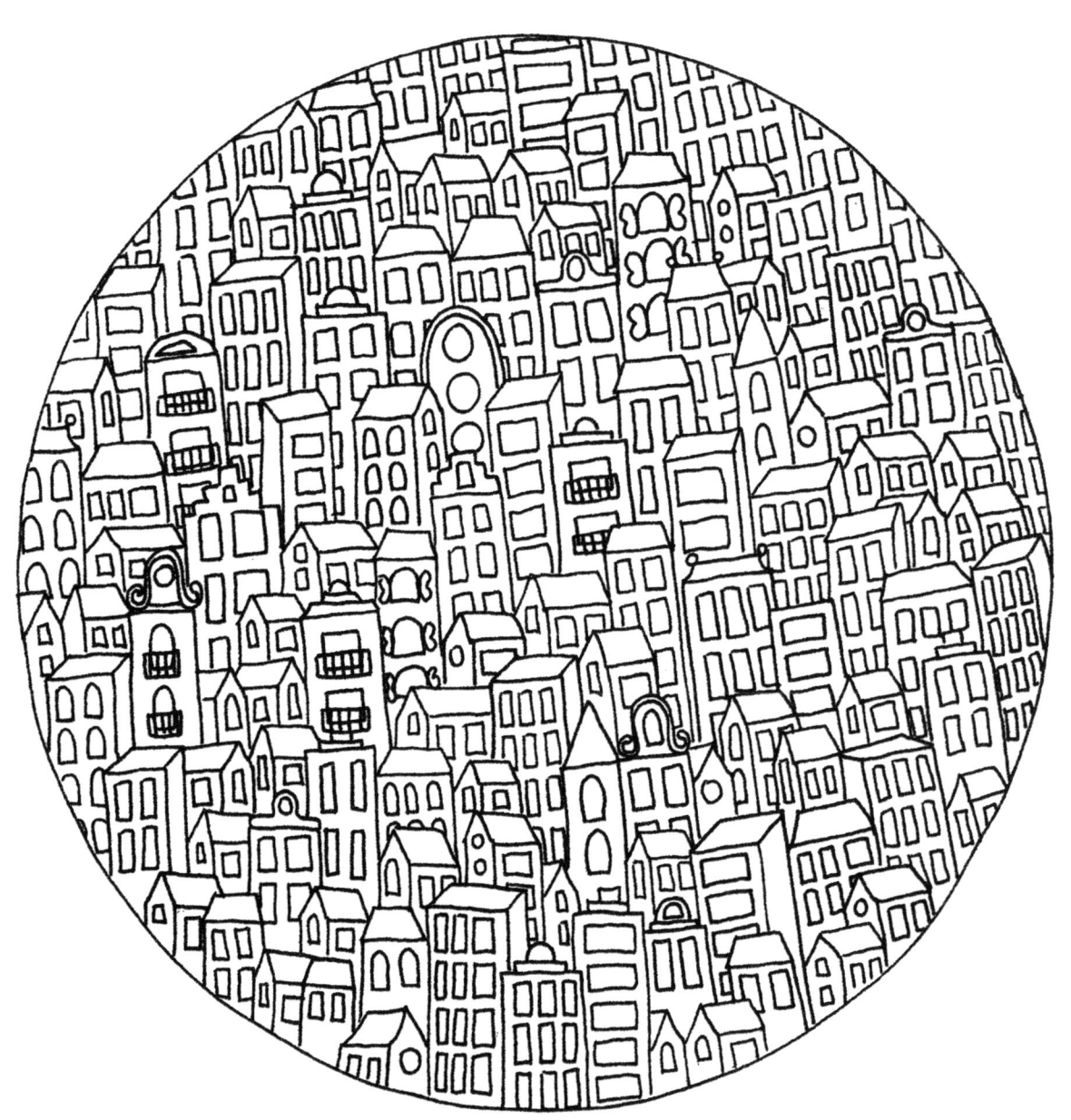

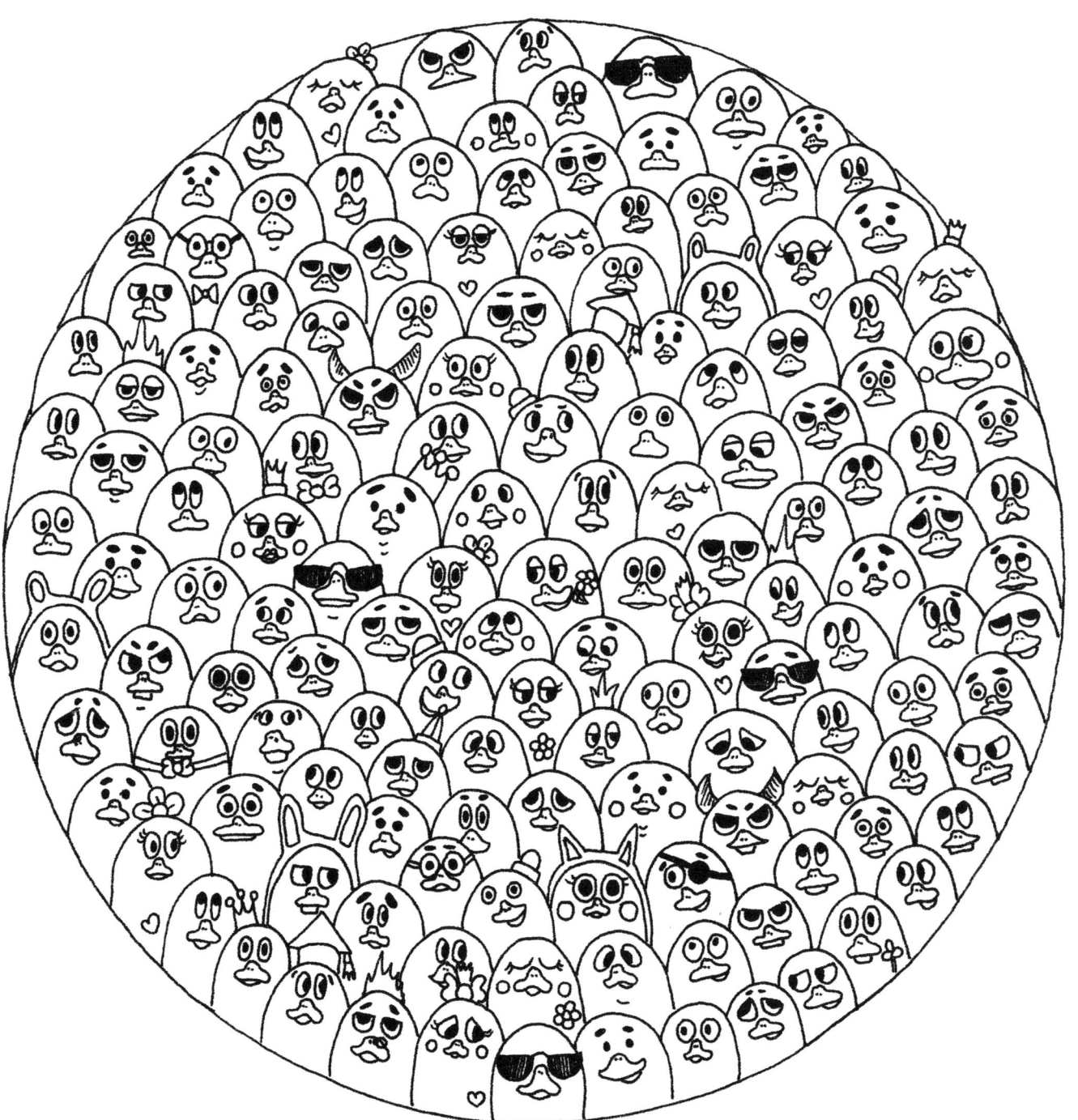

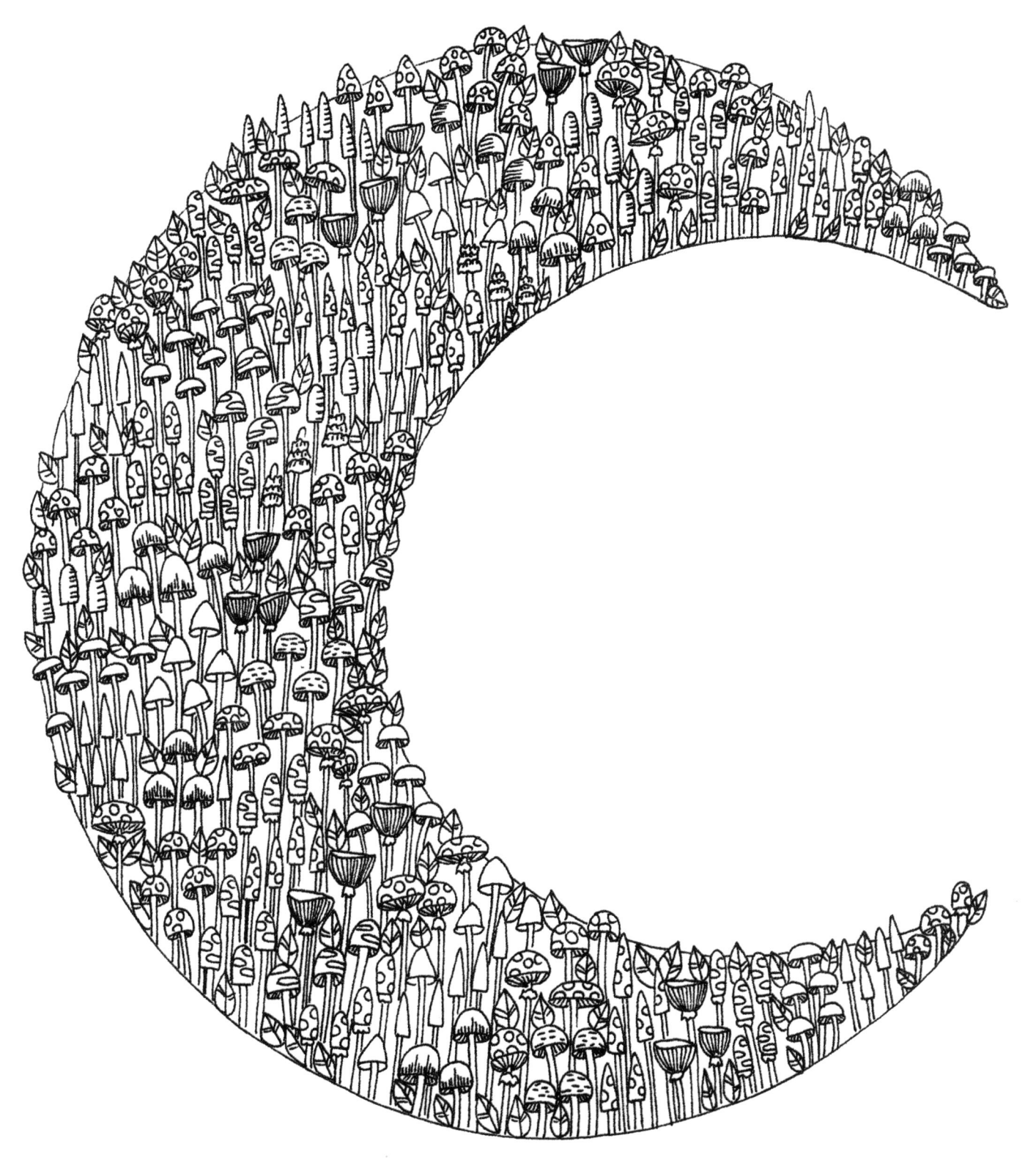

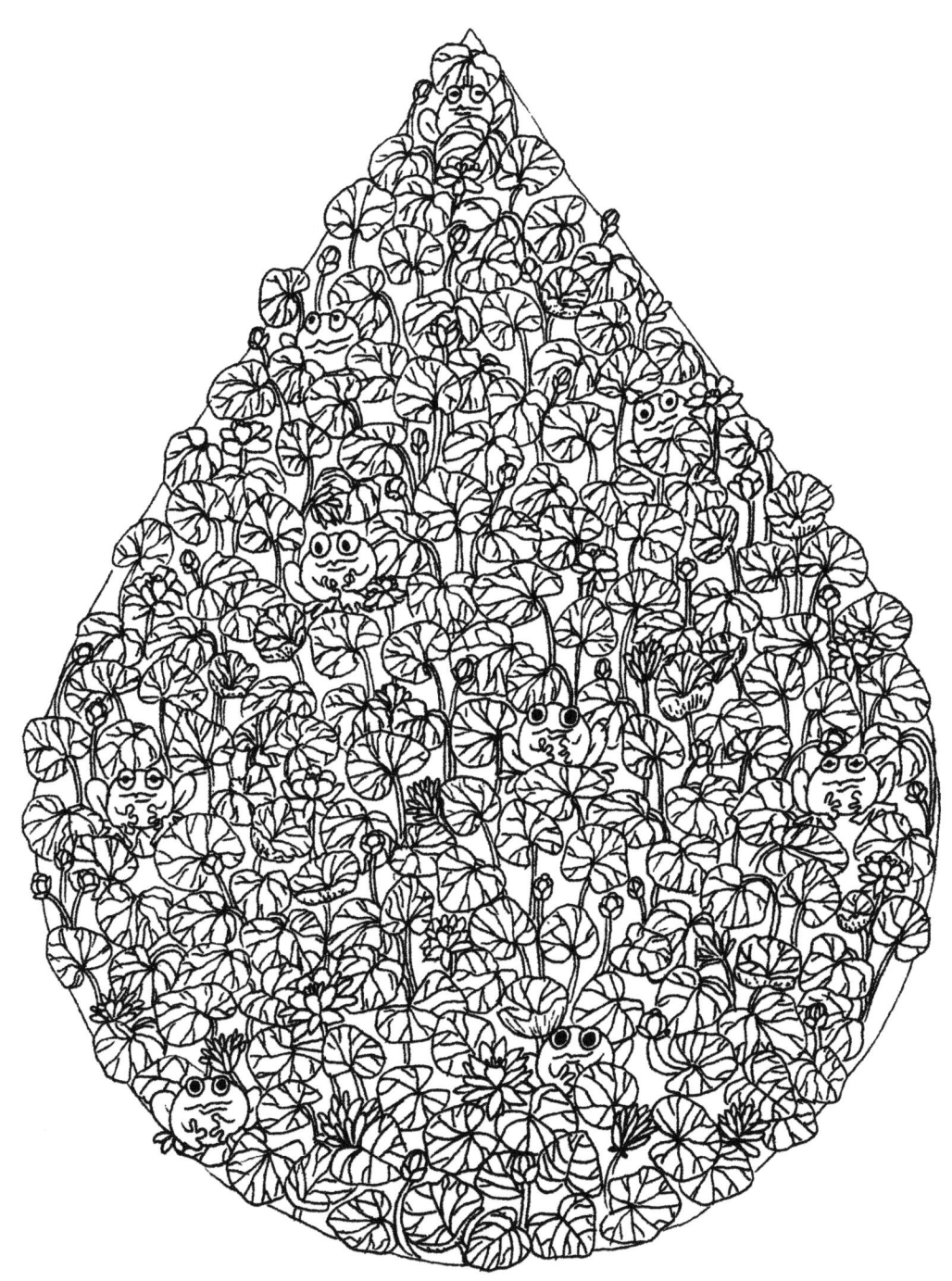

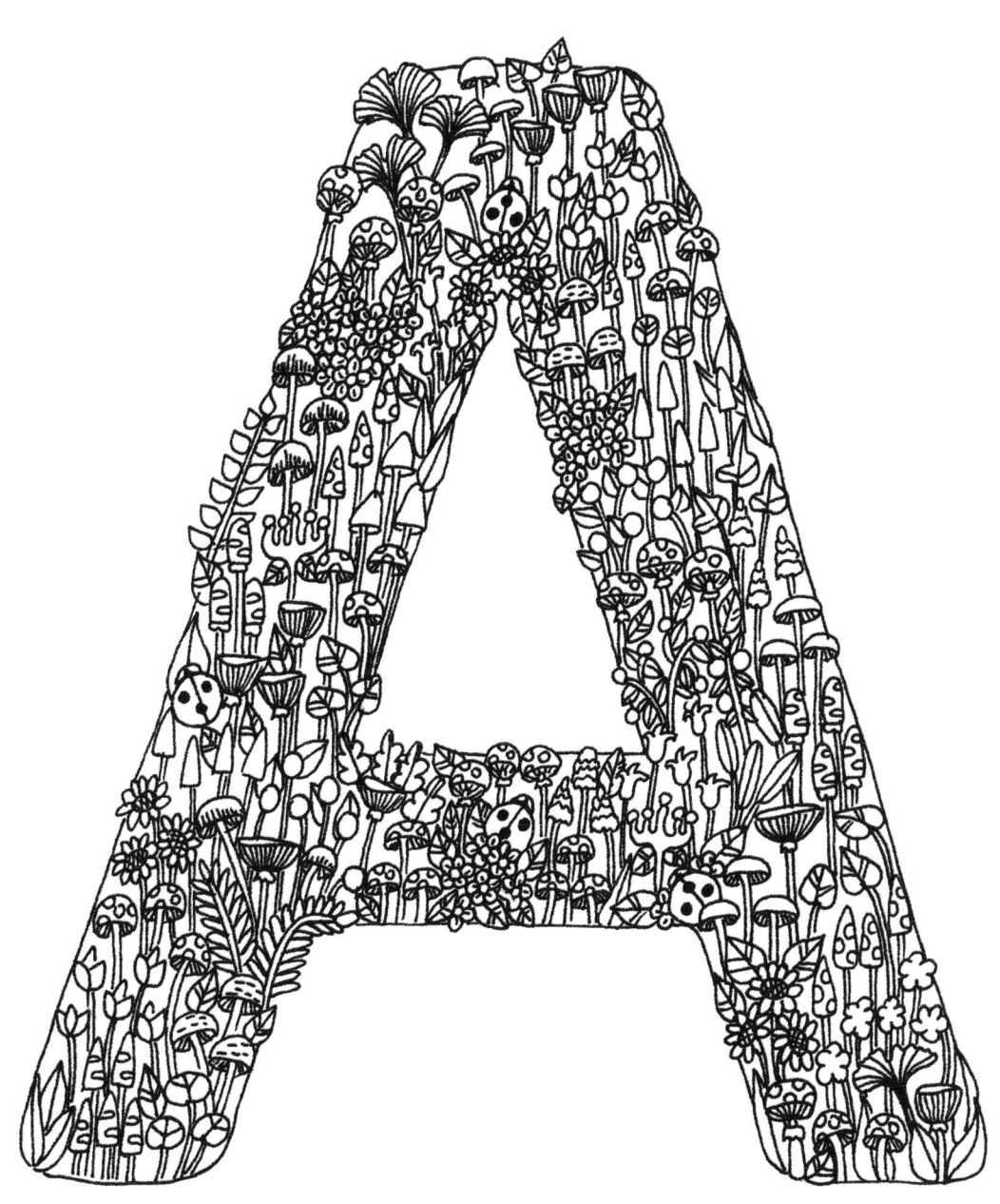

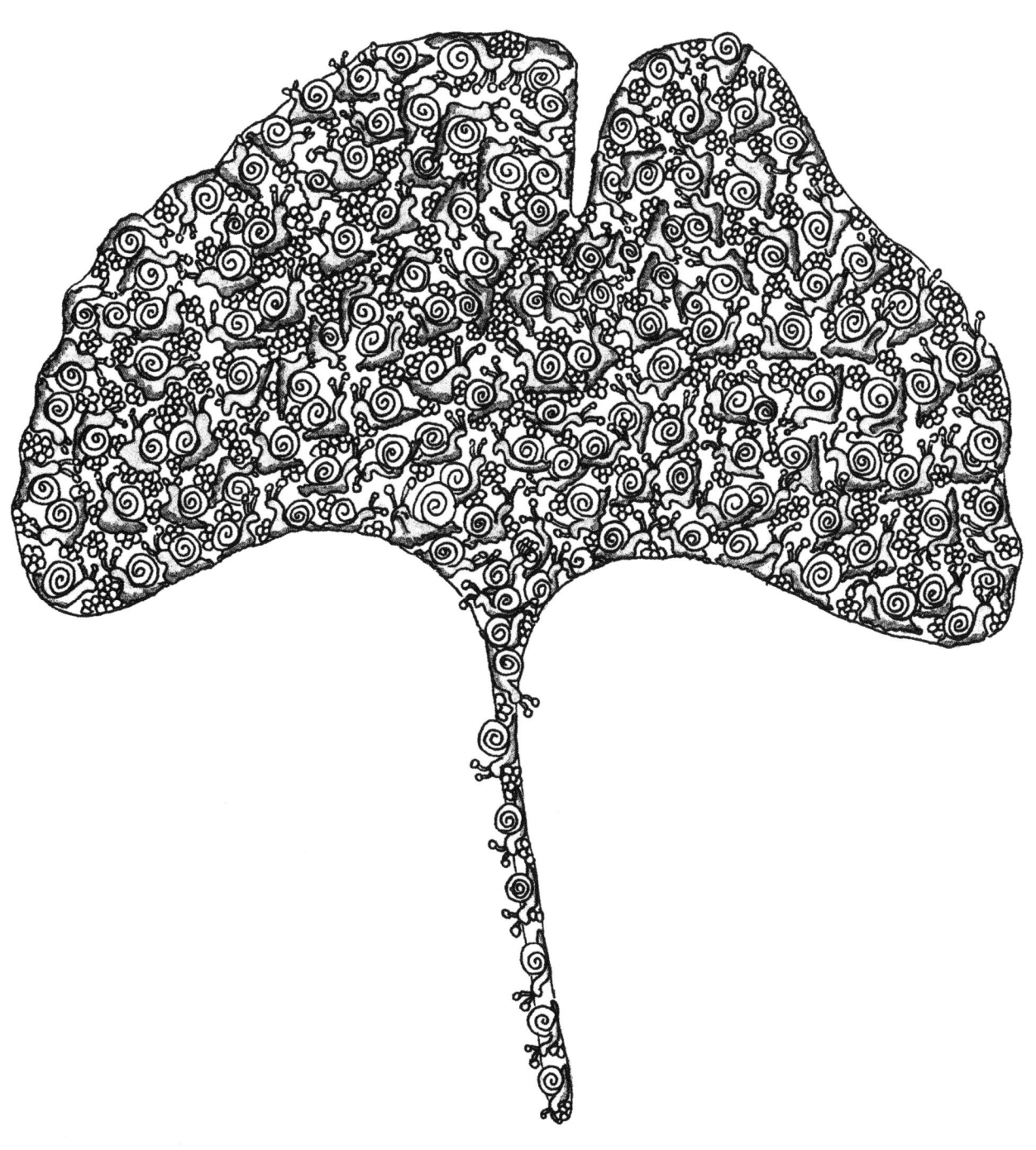

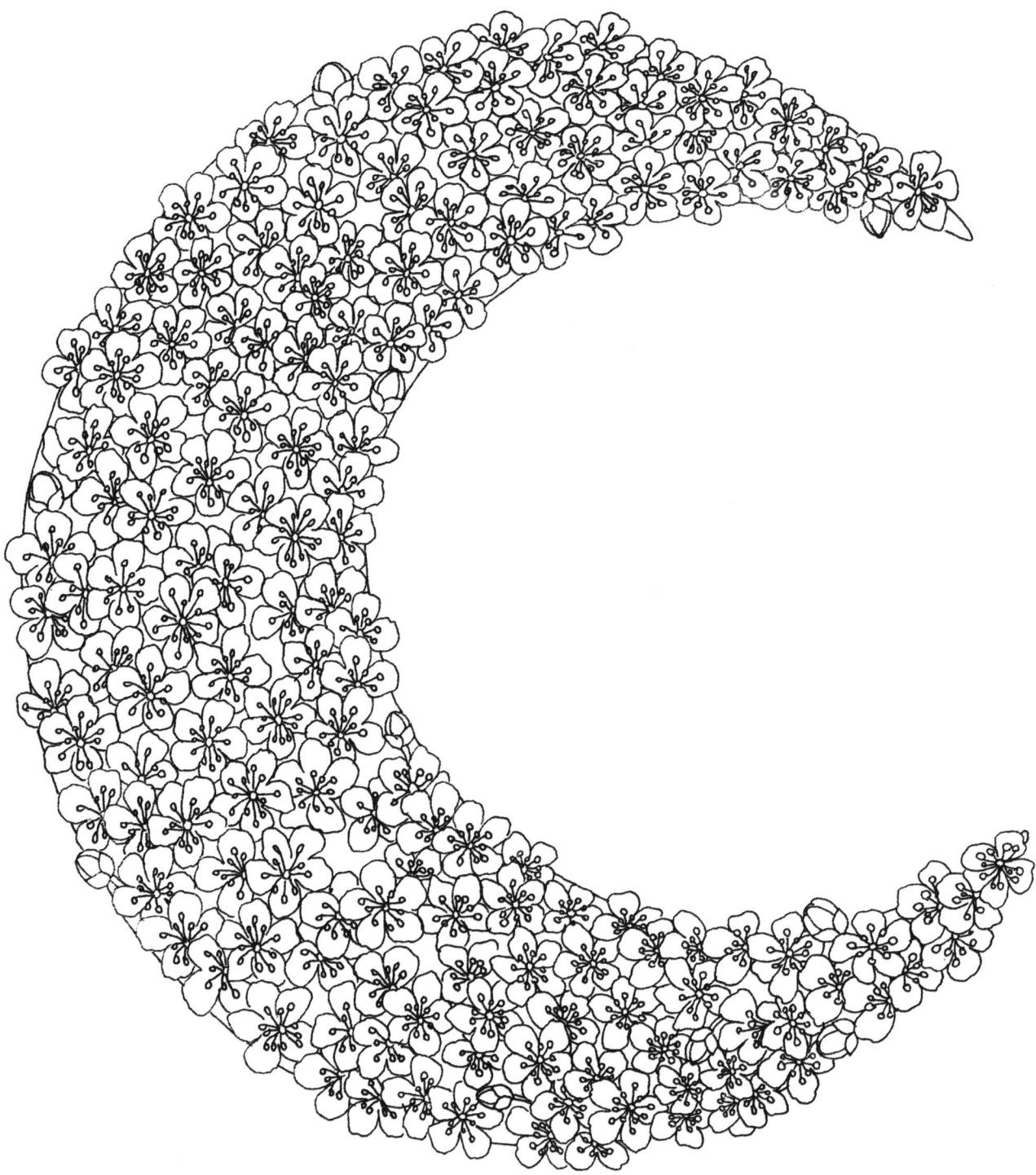

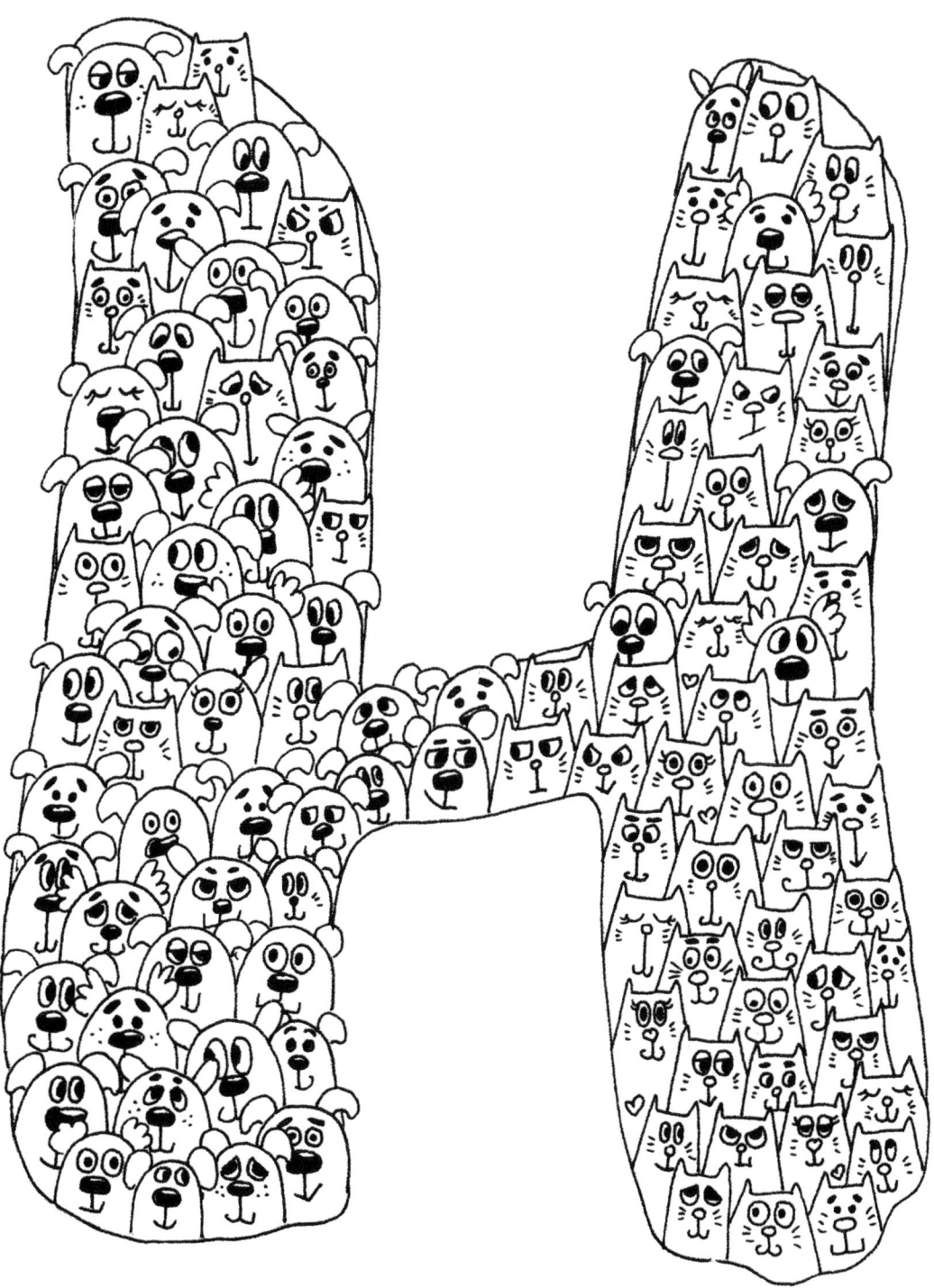

Acknowledgments

Most of all, I would like to thank Jo, who found me among thousands of wonderful artists. Without her, this book would not have been possible. Special thanks also go to Ella and her team, who provided tireless support and inspiration during development.

Thanks to my loved ones who supported and encouraged me in moments of doubt during my creative work. Without them, my world would look completely colorless and sad.

Thanks to everyone who faithfully supports me on social media. You are my best critics, who support me in a world of millions of artists.

Find out more

Anna Tjalsma-Pogorzelec (known online as Licosmoss) is a self-taught artist based in the Netherlands. Her intricate drawings, inspired by nature and childhood memories, have garnered a huge following on social media. Anna believes that with patience and practice anyone can draw, and she has written this book to encourage everyone to get creative and have fun with art.

If you want to see more of Anna's work and learn about her drawing process—including demonstrations of several different drawing and coloring techniques, from lines to dots and even miniatures—you can find her on Instagram and TikTok @licosmoss.